OLD TESTAMENT LAW FOR BIBLE STUDENTS

THE MACMILLAN COMPANY
NEW YORK · BOSTON · CHICAGO · DALLAS
ATLANTA · SAN FRANCISCO

MACMILLAN & CO., LIMITED
LONDON · BOMBAY · CALCUTTA
MELBOURNE

THE MACMILLAN CO. OF CANADA, LTD.
TORONTO

OLD TESTAMENT LAW FOR BIBLE STUDENTS

Classified and Arranged as in Modern Legal Systems

BY

ROGER SHERMAN GALER, A.M.
ATTORNEY-AT-LAW
AUTHOR OF "A LAYMAN'S RELIGION"

New York
THE MACMILLAN COMPANY
1922

Set up and printed. Published October, 1922

PRINTED IN THE UNITED STATES OF AMERICA

TO THE MEMBERS

OF

MY BIBLE CLASS,

TO WHOSE STUDIES

IN THE OLD TESTAMENT

JOINTLY WITH MY OWN,

THIS BOOK OWES

ITS ORIGIN

PREFACE

The study of that part of the Old Testament known as the Torah, or the Law, has usually been regarded as uninviting and unprofitable. The beginnings of the Torah consisted sometimes of single rules, sometimes of more or less related commands designated as statutes, or ordinances, of which the Ten Commandments are a familiar illustration. In time these various regulations were compiled as codes or definitive bodies of laws, and were united together with little regard for chronology or system. The result is confusing and it is little wonder that a systematic study of these laws has been impossible to any but trained Bible students. Few, if any, attempts have been made to render these laws readily accessible by reducing them to proper order both chronological and logical. The purpose of this book is to classify and arrange all the laws which constituted the Torah in accordance with the scheme of classification used in modern law books, whereby each topic or branch of the law is treated separately under appropriate subdivisions, and with all provisions relating to each subject grouped together. In this way the student has before him a complete analysis of the whole body of the Torah, into appropriate classes and divisions, such as the Rights and Privileges of Citizens, Courts and Legal Procedure, Domestic Relations, Laws of Inheritance, Laws Relating to Real Property, Criminal Law with its various branches, Religious Duties and Prohibitions, Humane Laws, and the large field of Ceremonial Law, including the various Feasts, Sacrifices, Law of Clean and Unclean, and Sacred Places and Persons.

Each of these classes is given a suitable analysis into its minor divisions, and every rule, command or law found in the Old Testament is grouped so as to furnish a complete picture of the law of ancient Israel on the particular subject.

The plan used in law books has also been adopted of stating a proposition or rule of law and following it with the supporting citation or Biblical text.

A constant comparison of the ancient Jewish law with modern statutes and codes will reveal a wonderful similarity in basic principles. The parallels are numerous and striking. A study of these cannot fail to be instructive, and will reveal unlooked-for phases of that living, human story which has persisted in all races and ages of the world's history.

Especial attention is directed to the Topical Index or Digest which is exhaustive of the various branches of the Law and which will furnish an invaluable key to systematic study. The Law thus becomes readily available to the average reader and Sunday school scholar, as well as to theological students. To active ministers the book should prove a work of ready reference which will save much time and research.

It is believed the plan outlined will remove many of the traditional difficulties in the study of Old Testament Law and make such study of intense interest and value.

Mt. Pleasant, Iowa, September, 1922.

CONTENTS

TOPICAL INDEX AND DIGEST

PUBLIC LAW

A

CIVIL GOVERNMENT

Kinds of Government

B

MILITARY LAWS

C

COURTS AND LEGAL PROCEDURE

Explanatory Note

PRIVATE LAW

A

CIVIL LAW

I

Domestic Relations

II

Laws of Inheritance

III

IV

V

VI

VII

VIII

B

B

C

D

E

F

G

H

ABBREVIATIONS USED

The American Revised Version (1901) is used for all references to the Old Testament.

Gen. = Genesis.
Ex. = Exodus.
Lev. = Leviticus.
Nu. = Numbers.
Dt. = Deuteronomy.
Jos. = Joshua.
Ju. = Judges.
S. or Sam. = Samuel.
K. = Kings.
Chr. = Chronicles.
Neh. = Nehemiah.
Ez. = Ezra.
Ps. = Psalms.
Pr. = Proverbs.
Is. = Isaiah.
Jer. = Jeremiah.
Ezek. = Ezekiel.
Am. = Amos.
Mic. = Micah.
Mac. = Maccabees.

INTRODUCTION

A

THE STUDY OF LEGAL ORIGINS

The study of a nation's history and traditions has always been regarded as of great significance. In an especial sense this truth is applicable to the study of legal origins. Cultural development and growth in the fundamental ideas of justice and humanity are perhaps better illustrated in the laws of a people than in any other one thing. The genius of a people, their most intimate thought, their very life blood, are crystallized in their laws.

The study of Israel's origins is not only interesting in itself, but these origins acquire an enhanced importance from the growth of religious ideas which they illustrate. How a small Semitic tribe through long wanderings in the desert and countless hardships developed the highest conception of God and the noblest religious literature of the ancient world is a strange and thrilling story, of the most absorbing interest. We find there the gradual growth of pure monotheism, the eloquence of prophets, the codes of law-givers, the persistent urge toward a nobler religious utterance, which cannot be matched in any other story, either ancient or modern. Our own religious notions are derived directly from this insignificant tribe in an obscure corner of the ancient civilized world. Surely we may study the early history of this race with profit. Many of our own laws no doubt had their remote progenitors in Judea. And the study of these historic foundations may, by proper methods of teaching, be made of absorbing interest to the youth who throng our schools.

In recent years Archæology has become one of the most important and valuable of sciences. Wonderful are the treasures unearthed by numerous expeditions which have been fitted out at great expense to explore the sites of buried cities. To these patient explorers nearly every country in the East has yielded its riches, and our knowledge of ancient life has been immeasurably increased in this way. The story of these expeditions and a description of the results obtained constitute one of the most fascinating chapters in modern scholarship. In many instances the Bible narrative has been corroborated by these newest of revelations. In nearly every case they are of the most absorbing interest to the student of history, throwing special light on the origin not only of laws, but of modes of thought and habits of living which afford us a fairly accurate knowledge of ancient life.

Fresh proof has also been furnished by these studies of the way in which laws come into being. Instead of sudden revelations or the promulgation of fully developed codes they show us that laws have their evolution; they grow out of the soil of national conditions, both physical and racial, such as climate, geographical position, rainfall, occupation and national temperament and ideals. These determine almost automatically the legal regulations which shall be established, and how these regulations shall change with changing conditions of national life. If a nation is largely agricultural the laws will relate chiefly to the tenure of land, its cultivation and the distribution of its products, and the contracts necessary to foster and encourage the tilling of the soil and the raising of domestic animals. Religious ceremonies will likewise relate largely to feasts of the seasons, determined by crop periods, and astronomical occurrences.

Such was the life of the ancient Jews. They were almost wholly nomads in their earlier history, farmers and herdsmen after they settled in Canaan. Both their laws and religion were determined by these facts, as the following pages will amply illustrate. The careful reader will also note, what indeed is inevitable, that the Jews had few laws relating to trade and commerce. The Jews were not a trading people and had little need for commercial or maritime law. They had no ships with which to trade with Alexandria or Tarshish; no caravans to cross the Syrian desert to Nineveh or Ur. Their habits of life were simple, their occupations few, their needs small. And their laws were an exact reflex of these dominant features in their national character and life.

There is still another fact which should be observed by the student of history. Laws follow national development instead of preceding it. Laws grow out of the needs of a people; they are made to preserve rights already acquired and to prevent new wrongs and injustice that may be devised. They cannot anticipate the direction or rate of growth of national needs. Rarely if ever has a ready-made code of laws been imposed upon a people by a higher power with any success. The complex conditions of society cannot be met by preconceived theories. Laws must follow the national consciousness and instinct, struggling as that instinct does with ever new conditions and unexpected wants. Laws thus enacted clothe a people as a garment and are necessarily and wisely conservative.

Examine carefully Jewish law at any stage of the national history and you will know the conditions in which the Jews lived in the preceding age with almost the certainty of a mathematical demonstration.

The Law, representing as it did the national ideals and instinct, and changing as it did with national needs, thus became the bond which held the Jewish race together as with bands of iron through all the varied centuries of national existence.

B

KINDS OF LAWS

Suppose a new invention such as the aeroplane comes into existence. At once new problems arise for solution. Who may operate the new machines? What rules shall regulate their passage over cities or the open fields? Who shall be held responsible for damage caused by collision or accident? Out of these and other conditions there will gradually emerge certain rules for the safe operation of aeroplanes which in time will be crystallized into custom. In the legal conflicts that will inevitably follow the courts will recognize these customs so far as they are founded upon justice and new rules will be laid down in their decisions. These precedents will be followed by courts in other cases until they become the well-settled law. Some of these will be enacted into statute law by local legislatures, or the national law making power. Ultimately the whole body of decisions, customs and statutes will be arranged into an orderly system. This will constitute a code. In such a way have grown up the great codes which in modern times govern the most important operations of modern states. They represent the final consensus of opinion of society on a given subject, its highest concept of right and justice. From facts to laws, this is the normal way in which society spins its laws out of its needs and conditions.

This same process is apparent in ancient Israel. There are at least four distinct strata of laws visible in the Pentateuch. New conditions arose, new laws were framed and were gradually compiled into codes, to which a great sanction was devised and added, the authority of Moses. There must be from time to time re-codifications of the law, to embody changed conditions, to meet new requirements, to eliminate contradictions, and to introduce harmony in procedure as well as the letter of the Law. In modern states there is sometimes added to the foregoing a Constitution, an underlying body of fundamental law, deemed of such vital importance that change and amendment are made very difficult.

Custom, precedent, statute, code, constitution, these are the various kinds of laws men have framed to protect them in their rights, and to redress or prevent wrong. The above is the order in which they are usually developed.

C

JEWISH DEBT TO BABYLONIAN LAWS

1

Recent archæological discoveries have shown a remarkable similarity between the legal codes of the Babylonian Semites and those of the Semitic Hebrews. Abraham migrated from Ur about five hundred years after the Code of Hammurabi was promulgated. How much of Babylonian laws he took with him is purely conjectural. It is also unknown to what extent the occasional commerce between Babylonia and Palestine prior to the Babylonian captivity had taken over the ideas, customs and laws of the older civilization. Certain it is that a high civilization had developed in the valleys of the Euphrates and Tigris two or three thousand years before the Hebrews were anything more than a race of nomads, with no settled home, habits or laws. What has excited the curiosity of scholars has been certain similarities in the form of traditions and stories especially those of the Creation of Man, the Origin of Sin and the Deluge.

There is a Babylonian story of Creation which furnishes a striking parallel to the Biblical story or rather stories of creation found in Genesis. Since the discovery of the former on cuneiform tablets in the library of Ashurbanipal in 1872 speculation has been rife among scholars as to the dependence of one on the other. The cosmogonies of the two races as illustrated by these legends are almost identical, though differing much in detail. The resemblances are much more numerous and striking than the differences. The Babylonian tradition as embodied in the epic of Marduk and Ti-Amat is of course vastly more ancient than that of the Hebrews and it is almost a logical necessity to conclude that the latter was taken in its essential features from the former. How traditions traveled over the ancient Eastern world from one country to another is just beginning to be appreciated. There must have been a much more cosmopolitan exchange of ideas and culture than their comparative isolation has heretofore led us to believe. Oral tradition, the intellectual vehicle in oriental countries, preserves knowledge from generation to generation, and is persistently long lived in countries where written language is confined to the few, and where the conflicting interests of a complex civilization are unknown.

The Gilgamesh epic is another famous story which dates at least as far back as 3000 B. C. It is a legend of a great flood which destroyed most of the human race but from which Ut-Napishtim, the ancestor of Gilgamesh, was saved by building a ship into which he took all his possessions and seed of life of every kind. After seven days the rains ceased, the ship grounded, a dove was sent out to find land, and finally all the animals were landed, and Bel the great god was pacified and made a covenant with the race of men. The resemblance to the Bible story is so marked in all its details that it is highly probable that the Babylonian legend persisted through centuries of oral repetition and was adopted by the authors of Genesis.

There is little external evidence of any direct transfer of ideas, culture or laws in the early days of the Hebrew occupation of Canaan. But the internal evidence in the matter of laws of a common origin of Jewish and Babylonian law is such as to provoke the serious attention of scholars. Differences there were in racial temperament, conditions and environment. Yet the laws of the two countries developed many of the same ideas as to the rights of property, modes of punishment, and regulations for the conduct of business. It seems reasonable to infer the Jews borrowed from the older and more highly developed civilization. Possibly their borrowings came through the medium of the Canaanites—the inhabitants of Palestine at the time of the Jewish invasion. The whole story of the debt of Israel to Babylonia in laws, traditions and religious ideas is a most fascinating one which cannot be discussed fully within the limits of this work.

When Palestine was overrun by Assyrian and Babylonian and Persian conquerors the Jews came under the direct and powerful influence of these higher civilizations. The later Jewish Codes were affected greatly by this contact in at least two ways. One was by direct comparison and imitation. The other was the result of the national tragedy, the intensification of the racial self-consciousness, and emphasis upon a spiritual career for a people who had lost their political independence.

Jewish laws as found in the Pentateuch bear incontrovertible internal evidence of evolution almost untouched by outside influences prior to this period of exile. The ear-marks of this evolution are plainly visible. The laws are such as would be naturally adapted to a primitive agricultural society, and primitive conceptions of religious truth. There is a gradual development of laws showing a more and more advanced state of social evolution. Religious conceptions too become more exalted, owing largely to the impassioned preaching of the prophets, a wonderful religious literature springs into existence, the lofty idea of Monotheism becomes firmly established. These religious conceptions of the prophets and this religious literature show but little evidence of any imported influence. They are characteristic of Jewish genius and peculiarly adapted to the circumstances under which the Jews lived. They display an instinct for religion, whatever may be the explanation of that fact, and the intense devotion of the Hebrews to religious ideals gave color and direction to their whole subsequent history.

2

The Code of Hammurabi above referred to is the oldest known code of laws, dating from the reign of that great monarch about 2100 B. C. Recent translations of the inscriptions on clay tablets found in Babylonian mounds indicate still older laws, probably those out of which the Hammurabic code was compiled. An ancient civilization, that of the Sumerians, the earliest known inhabitants of the great valley of the Euphrates, has been discovered, a civilization dating back to 5000 or 6000 years B. C. But little is known of their legal systems. It is probable, however, that the Babylonians inherited from the Sumerians some of their customs, religious concepts, perhaps legal institutions. A prominent feature of the Hammurabic Code is quite apparent. It indicates a commercial civilization. There were merchants and traders, notaries, lawyers, judges, a commercial code, laws relating to interest, rents, lands, servants. It discloses also a material civilization. And this is true despite the fact that there were some evidences of a high standard for that day of morals and ethics relating to marriage and divorce, the rights of women, of foreigners and slaves. Religious conceptions of course were primitive as viewed in the light of to-day. And yet Babylonian gods were represented as favoring justice and as demanding of rulers kindness to their subjects. On the whole a much higher level of civilization and a much more complex organization of society are illustrated by the Hammurabic Code than by the corresponding legislation of the Hebrews, always bearing in mind the nobler conceptions of the latter as to the nature of Jehovah and his relation to his human creatures.

3

One of the distinctions to be noted between Babylonian and Jewish law is that the former was almost wholly secular, while the latter soon engaged itself with humane and religious conceptions. Indeed the Code of Hammurabi related largely to trade and commerce, and hence had much to do with real and personal property, contracts, prices of commodities, rules for the sale and exchange of goods, leases of land, prices of labor, interest, bailments, and cost of transporting merchandise, all of which were minutely regulated by law. It also included injuries to property and those criminal offenses that arose out of this intense commercial life, such as theft, robbery, embezzlement, cheating and fraud of various kinds. Domestic relations were regulated in accordance with the moral standards in force in this prosperous and opulent community. There were almost no laws involving moral or humane conceptions. It was left to the Jews to leave the customary path of laws relating only to property and crimes, and introduce the human element into their legal systems. Indeed it may be regarded as the chief distinguishing mark as it is the peculiar glory of the Jewish race to place the emphasis of the law upon persons rather than property.

Commercial activity produces definite and precise laws regulating trade usages and conditions. Written contracts contained the record of commercial transactions and thousands of clay tablets, discovered in buried libraries, palaces and temples in Babylonia, exhibit a complex civilization and a highly developed legal system. The "law merchant" became the basis of the commercial law of England and America; in like manner the customs of merchants and shippers in Babylonia were crystallized in that code of Hammurabi which is one of the most splendid and illuminating pages that have been preserved for us out of the night of ancient history.[1]

D

THE TORAH

Definition, History and Constituent Codes

The Old Testament consists of three great parts or divisions—the Law, the Prophets, and the Wisdom Writings or Hagiographa. These were united in their present form about 90 to 100 A. D. The first of these divisions, the Torah, is for the Jews the most sacred, the very heart and essence of the Old Testament. Wherever the Law is spoken of either in the old or new Testaments, the Torah is meant. It was the Torah which according to tradition was given to Moses amid the thunders and lightnings of Sinai. It was the Torah to which Christ had reference when he spoke of the law as handed down by Moses. The Torah contained the moral rules of conduct and the religious ceremonial which all Jews must observe, as well as civil and criminal regulations. And it was the Torah which gave rise to the different schools of interpretation, and the great body of comment and decisions known as the Talmud.

The Law is not a single Code, but is made up of miscellaneous statutes and of several codes formulated at different times under varying conditions. There is little doubt that the Pentateuch was edited by later redactors who took existing laws and arranged them in their present order. The process was sometimes unskillfully done and the result is a mass of material with little coherence or unity. When the various laws are dug out of the quarries of narrative, of repetition, of allegory and tra-

[1] For a further study of Babylonian law see John's translation of the Code of Hammurabi.

dition in which they are embedded they reveal different strata, each of which has its own unity of structure and purpose.

During all the period when these laws were formulated the Jews were essentially a theocracy. We must not expect to find in the Torah a complete code of civil and criminal laws in the modern sense of the term. Most Jewish laws were religious in their character. Civil government as understood at present was almost unknown. There was no specially constituted legislative body as in modern states chosen for the sole purpose of making laws. Legislative, judicial and executive power were all lodged in the same persons. The Jews were a primitive people with little or no commerce, with no large cities, but little accumulated wealth, and with the transfer of land on any considerable scale prohibited by law. No scheme of classification such as is used in modern times is exactly applicable to the Jewish system of laws. Scholars are able to point out in different parts of the Pentateuch various bodies of laws each of which had in its time an independent existence, and which developed under different conditions in various periods of Jewish history. Clearly marked these are, their boundary lines being for the most part easily distinguishable. The idea of uniformity which once prevailed as to the Bible story has been dissipated by the results of modern Biblical scholarship.

These various bodies of laws were not codified by a commission of experts. The fact that laws are repeated in the different codes proves they were not formulated by a single lawgiver. Often there are contradictions, as for instance where various places of sacrifice are commanded as in Ex. 20[24] and at Jerusalem only as in Dt. 12. No copies of the laws were at first made; they consisted of oral decisions and precepts, handed down from one generation to the next. Later they were committed to writing, probably on tables of stone. Ex. 24[4], 31[18], 32[16], 34[27, 28].

The Deuteronomic Code was compiled or at least written down in its present form about 621 B. C., the Priestly Code in the fifth century B. C. The first legislation is probably found in Ex. 18[14-16], where according to tradition Moses found it necessary to formulate rules for the decision of disputed questions, and to appoint stated persons to whom such questions could be submitted. Ex. 18[19-22, 25, 26.] This is undoubtedly the foundation of Hebrew Law. Decisions made in this way really constituted legislation, there being no other authority to make rules for the guidance of the people. The precedent of judicial decisions crystallizing into a great body of positive law finds a signal modern illustration in the common law of England, which had its origin in the decisions of the courts, but which has all the force and authority of laws expressly enacted by Parliament, in the particular fields in which it is applicable.

There is another consideration that must be kept constantly in mind. As each new code was formulated its compilers gave it vast authority by ascribing it to Moses. This constant reference of new regulations to Moses is everywhere visible. Without the sanction of his name the laws would have had but little force. It was difficult even by the help of his overshadowing authority to secure their observance. Very often the Jews were called a stiff-necked and rebellious people. This does not mean of course that all Jewish law came into being after Moses had died. No doubt there were many primitive regulations that had their origin during the wanderings in the desert, when Moses was their leader and lawgiver. We may look here for the germ of later codes. Perhaps the central core of the Ten Commandments came out of the intense experience of their early travails and misfortunes. The law of retaliation was no doubt then in actual use. Some primitive civil regulations may have developed. But the elaboration of these into code and established doctrine could happen only after later experiences and more complex conditions of life and environment. It must be remembered too that anthropomorphic ideas were common among the Jews in their earliest period. Jehovah was to them a big, glorified person, having many of the human instincts, passions, impulses. He loved his people and hated their enemies. The Israelites were his chosen people. When he spoke to them it was with visible presence, an audible voice, lightnings and thunderings, tables of stone. They were impressed by his awful majesty, which was real to them only when accompanied by these material manifestations of his power and presence.

In the light of the foregoing considerations the Jewish laws should be studied. We may establish a correct chronology of the various codes, study their real content, learn of the conditions under which they were formulated, and thus obtain a true picture of their meaning and worth to us. Let us proceed in this spirit with the study of these individual codes.

Constituent Elements of the Torah and Their Designations

We shall refer frequently to the letters J.E.C.D.H. and P. An explanation of these is necessary.

Scholars have long recognized that the Pentateuch is not a literary unit but is made up of various elements which were united by later editors into its present form. Higher Criticism has studied this part of the Old Testament exhaustively and has reached conclusions that are fairly harmonious and generally accepted. It is agreed for instance that there is a stream of narrative or history running through the Pentateuch, which has well defined characteristics as a rule easily recognized, and which habitually uses the term Jehovah to designate God. This constituent element is by common consent represented by the letter J. Parallel to this and united with it to make up the present form of the historic narrative is another element characterized by the use of the term Elohim and hence designated as E. These were united by a later editor into those portions of the Pentateuch known as JE. There came much later an addition of priestly narrative, for the most part easily distinguishable, designated as the Priest's Code by the letter P. Into these welded narratives were thrown certain more or less homogeneous bodies of laws known respectively as C, D, and H. These are explained fully in subsequent sections. As a convenient summary of these elements we submit the following tables taken from Driver, which represent better perhaps than any other the deliberate judgment of scholars as to the make-up of the Torah.[1]

"J"

Genesis 2^{4b} to 3^{24}, 4^{1-26}, 5^{29}, $6^{1-4, 5-8}$, $7^{1-5, 7-10, 12, 16b-17b, 22-23}$, $8^{2b-3a, 6-12, 13b, 20-22}$, 9^{18-27}, $10^{8-19, 21, 24-30}$, $11^{1-9, 28-30}$, $12^{1-4a, 6-20}$, $13^{1-5, 7-11a, 12b, 13-18}$, $16^{1b-2, 4-14}$, 18^{1} to $19^{28, 30-38}$, $21^{1a-2a, 33}$, $22^{15-18, 20-24}$, 24^{All}, $25^{1-6, 11b, 18, 21-26, 27-34}$, $26^{1-14, 16-17, 19-33}$, 27^{1-45}, $28^{10, 13-16, 19}$, $29^{2-14, 31-35}$, $30^{3b-5, 7, 9-16, 20b, 22b, 24}$ to $31^{1, 3, 46, 48-50}$, $32^{3-13a, 22, 24-32}$, 33^{1-17}, $34^{2b-3, 5, 7, 11, 12, 19, 25, 26, 30, 31}$, $35^{14, 21, 22a}$, $37^{12-18, 21, 25-27, 28b, 31-35}$, c38, c39, 42^{38}-44^{34}, 46^{28}-$47^{4, 6b}$, $47^{13-26, 27a, 29-31}$, $49^{1b \text{ to } 28a}$, $50^{1-11, 14}$.

Exodus $1^{6, 8-12, 20b, 15-23a}$, $3^{2-4a, 5, 7-8, 16-18}$, 4^{1-16}, $4^{19-20a, 22-26, 29-31}$, $5^{3, 5-23}$, 6^{1}, $7^{14-15a, 16, 17, 18, 20c-21a}$, 7^{23-25}, $8^{1-4, 8-15a, 20-32}$, $9^{1-7, 13-21, 23b, 24b, 25b-34}$, 10^{1-11}, $10^{13b, 14b-15a, 15c-19, 24-26, 28-29}$, 11^{4-8}, 12^{29f}, $13^{3-16, 21f}$, $14^{5-7, 10a, 11-14, 19b-20, 21b, 24-25, 27b, 30-31}$, 15^{22-27}, 16^{4-5}, 16^{25-30}, $17^{1b-2, 7}$, $19^{3b-9, 11b-13, 18, 20-25}$, $24^{1-2, 9-11}$, 32^{25-34}, $33^{1-4, 12-23}$, $34^{1-4, 5-28}$.

Numbers 10^{29-36}, 12^{16}.

[1] These citations are from Driver's *Introduction to the Literature of the Old Testament*, by permission of the publishers, Charles Scribner's Sons, New York.

"E"

Genesis 15 ^{Chapter}, 20^{1-17}, $21^{6-21,\ 22-32a}$, $22^{1-14,\ 19}$, $28^{11,\ 12,\ 17,\ 18,\ 20-22}$, $29^{1,\ 15-23,\ 25-28,\ 30}$, $30^{1-3a,\ 6,\ 8}$, $30^{17-20a,\ 20c-22b,\ 23}$, $31^{2,\ 4-18a,\ 19-45,\ 47,\ 51\ \text{to}}$ $32^{2,\ 13b-21,\ 23}$, $33^{18b-20,}$ $35^{1-8,\ 16-20}$, $37^{2b,\ 3-11,\ 19-20,\ 22-24,\ 28a,\ 28a-30-36}$, c40, c $41^{1-45,\ 45-57}$, 42^{1-37}, 45^{1}-$46^{5,\ 12}$, $48^{1,\ 2,\ 8-22}$, $48^{15-26.}$

Exodus $1^{15-20a,\ 21-22}$, 2^{1-14}, $3^{1,\ 4b,\ 6,\ 9-15,\ 19-22}$, 4^{17-18}, $4^{20b-21,\ 27-28}$, $5^{1-2,\ 4}$, $7^{15b,\ 17,\ 20b}$, $9^{22-23a,\ 24a,\ 25a,\ 35}$, $10^{12-13a,\ 14a,\ 15b,\ 20,\ 21-23,\ 27}$, 11^{1-3}, $12^{31-36,\ 37b-39,\ 42a}$, 13^{17-19}, $14^{10b,\ 19a}$, $15^{1-18,\ 20-21}$, $17^{3-6,\ 8-16}$, 18^{chapter}, $19^{2b,\ 3a}$, $19^{10-11a,\ 14-17,\ 19}$, 20^{1-21}, 20^{22}-23^{33}, $24^{3-8,\ 12-14,\ 18b}$, 31^{18b}, $32^{1-8,\ 15-24,\ 35}$, $33^{5-6,\ 7-11.}$

Numbers 11^{1-3}, $12^{1-15.}$

"JE"

Exodus 12^{21-27}, 13^{3-16}, $32^{9-14.}$

Numbers 11^{4-35}, 13-14, 16, $20^{1-13,\ 14-21}$, $21^{1-3,\ 4-9,\ 10-20}$, 21^{21-32}, 22^{2}-24^{25}, $25^{1-5.}$

Deuteronomy 27^{5-7a}, $31^{14-15,\ 23}$, 33, $34^{1a,\ 1b-5a,\ 6,\ 10.}$

"P"

Genesis 1 to 2^{4a}, $5^{1-28,\ 30-32}$, 6^{9-22}, $7^{6,\ 11,\ 13-16a,\ 17a,\ 18-21,\ 24}$, $8^{1-2a,\ 3b-5,\ 13a,\ 14-19}$, $9^{1-17,\ 28-29}$, $10^{1-7,\ 20,\ 22-23,\ 31-32}$, $11^{10-26,\ 27,\ 31-32}$, 12^{4b-5}, $13^{6,\ 11b,\ 12a}$, $16^{1a,\ 3,\ 15-16}$, 17, 19^{29}, $21^{1b,\ 2b-5}$, 23, $25^{7-11a,\ 12-17,\ 19-20,\ 26b}$, 26^{34-35}, 27^{46} to 28^{9}, $29^{24,\ 29}$, 31^{18b}, 33^{18a}, $34^{1-2a,\ 4,\ 6,\ 8-10,\ 13-18,\ 20-24,\ 25,\ 27-29}$, $35^{9-13,\ 15,\ 22b-29}$, 36, 37^{1-2a}, 41^{46}, 46^{6-27}, $47^{5-6a,\ 7-11,\ 27b-28}$, $48^{3-6,\ 7}$, $49^{1a,\ 28b-33}$, $50^{12-13.}$

Exodus $1^{1-5,\ 7,\ 13-14}$, 2^{23b-25}, 6^{2}-$7^{13,\ 19-20a,\ 21b-22}$, $8^{5-7,\ 15b-19}$, 9^{8-12}, 11^{9-10}, $12^{1-20,\ 28,\ 37a,\ 40-41,\ 43-51}$, $13^{1-2,\ 20}$, $14^{1-4,\ 8-9,\ 15-18,\ 21a,\ 21c-23,\ 26-27a,\ 28a,\ 29}$, $16^{1-3,\ 6-24,\ 31-36}$, 17^{1a}, 19^{1-2a}, 24^{15-18a}, 25^{1}-31^{18a}, 34^{29-35}, 35-40.

Leviticus, Ch. 1-16 (Ch. 17-26), Ch. 27.

Numbers 1^{1}-$10^{28,\ 34}$, $13^{1-17a,\ 21,\ 25-26a,\ 32a}$, $14^{1-2,\ 5-7,\ 10,\ 26-30,\ 34-38}$, 15, $16^{1a,\ 2b-7a,\ (7b-11),\ (16-17),\ 18-24,\ 27a,\ 32b,\ 35,\ (36-40),\ 41-50}$, Ch. 17-19, $20^{1a,\ 2,\ 3b-4,\ 6-13,\ 22-29}$, $21^{4a,\ 10-11}$, 22^{1}, 25^{6-18}, Ch. 26-31, $32^{18-19,\ 28-32}$, Ch. 33-36.

Deuteronomy 1^{3}, 32^{48-52}, $34^{1a,\ 5b,\ 7a,\ 8-9.}$

"D"

Deuteronomy 1^{1-2}, 1^{4}-3^{13}, 3^{14-17}, 3^{18}-4^{28}, $4^{29-31,\ 32-40,\ 41-43,\ 44-49}$, 5^{1}-26^{19}, $27^{1-4,\ 7b-8,\ 9-10,\ 11-13,\ (14-26)}$, Ch. 28, $29^{1-6,\ 10-29}$, $30^{1-10,\ 11-20}$, $31^{1-13,\ (16-22),\ 24-27,\ 28-30}$, ($32^{1-43}$), $^{44,\ 45-47}$, $34^{11-12.}$

"C"

Exodus 20^{22} to $23^{33.}$

"H"

Leviticus 17-26.

1

The Book of the Covenant

Exodus 20^{22} to 23^{33}
Date about 800 B. C.

Hereafter in this volume the Book of the Covenant will be cited as C.

The oldest written Jewish law is probably that found in Exodus $34^{1, 4, 27, 28}$. It was a covenant between Jehovah and Israel. In Exodus $34^{18\text{-}28}$ we find the original form of the Ten Words which later became the familiar Decalogue. These became the core and essence of the Torah. In addition there were scattering regulations and decisions applicable to the primitive conditions of the times. At last these were gathered together into a code, the earliest compiled body of the Jewish law, about the year 800 B. C. This is called the Book of the Covenant, which is found in Exodus 20^{22} to 23^{33}. It immediately follows the Decalogue in the later edition named Exodus, and was so called because thus designated in Exodus 24^{7}.

The Book of the Covenant originally consisted of oral decisions and regulations, which were later written down, and became legal precedents and served as a handbook for judges. It presumes a primitive state of society in which agriculture was the principal occupation. The principles of justice in civil and criminal cases were quite simple, and religious conceptions were crude and undeveloped.

Even here, however, we note some refinements in legal classification, and in the various classes of crimes. The distinction between different degrees of murder, Exodus

21^{13-14}, is identical in principle with that of modern codes.

A few citations will illustrate the fact that the more common crimes were well recognized and provisions made for their punishment, while the more subtle refinements and distinctions of modern times were unknown.

Injuries not resulting in death..	Exodus	21^{16-32}
Injuries to cattle	"	21^{33-36}
Theft	"	22^{1-5}
Arson	"	22^{6}
Breach of trust	"	22^{7-13}
Seduction	"	22^{16-17}
Witchcraft	"	22^{18}

Practically all of civil and criminal law was embodied under two headings—retaliation, and pecuniary compensation. The Book of the Covenant contains no elements of commercial law.

2

The Book of the Law, or The Deuteronomic Code

Deuteronomy 5-11, 12-26 and other parts of Deuteronomy
Date 621 B. C.
(Cited as D)

Jewish worship throughout its whole history was based upon sacrifice. Jehovah's favor must be courted and his wrath appeased by the sacrifice of something of great value to the worshiper, the firstlings of his flocks and herds, the finest of his fruits and grains. In the early days there were "high places" in every community, usually the summits of hills, where Jehovah had "set his name," where these sacrifices might be offered. At first the worshiper himself might kill the victim and offer the oblation. Upon the altars of Jehovah smoked the victims of countless sacrifices. Later the ceremonial was performed by priests and the "high places" became established altars. In the reign of Josiah (639-600 B. C.) the abuses of this system of worship became intolerable. The high places became the scenes of the grossest immorality. All kinds of idolatry were practiced, and personal uncleanness abounded. The local priests were unable or unwilling to check the abuses. It was to meet this serious situation that the entire body of Israel's laws was collected into a code. In solemn manner it was announced to the people that the "Book of the Law" had been discovered while making repairs in the temple, 2 Kings 22, and that it dated back to Moses. This Book of the Law, it has been agreed by practically all scholars since Jerome, is the Deuteronomic Code, found in chapters 5 to 11 and 12 to 26 of Deuteronomy. It commanded the complete destruction of the old altars and sacred places scattered through Palestine. All worship was hereafter centered in the temple at Jerusalem. This made worship difficult and expensive to the common people, but it had the effect of doing away with many of the abuses that could be cured only by this drastic reform.

Henceforth the story of Jewish worship and culture centers in the temple. An elaborate ritual was the inevitable consequence. An extensive organization of priests, Levites and helpers sprang up at Jerusalem. All power and authority were vested in the priesthood, both religious and civil, and all the currents of Jewish life were reversed.

D, as the Deuteronomic Code will hereafter be referred to was an expansion of JE which was not yet united to P, and was undoubtedly a re-codification of all laws in force up to that time, including those in the Book of the Covenant. In this respect it may be compared to the Code of Justinian which summarized and codified all Roman law up to that time, and to the Code Napoleon, that splendid remolding of French law which constitutes one of the noblest monuments to the genius whose fame rests chiefly on his military exploits.

D presupposes a much higher civilization than that exhibited by C. Society was more highly developed, and new problems called for special laws. It also displays a much higher moral sense than C. It is written with a lofty eloquence which distinguishes it above most other parts of the Pentateuch. It emphasizes life and conduct rather than mere formal acts of sacrifice. It lays stress upon ethical ideas, and humane sentiments are common. In some of its provisions it contradicts, or at least supplants C. The latter, Exodus 20 ^{24}, commands the erection of altars at various places. D centers all religious functions at Jerusalem. It was not the work of a jurist, but a prophet. Very justly D may be regarded as being the high water-mark of ancient law, superior in its religious and humane conceptions, not only to all former Jewish law, but to the laws of any other ancient peoples of that period. Some scholars, including Jewish, assert there was a D ^{2} which added Deuteronomy 27, 29 $^{10-29}$, 30 $^{1-10}$ and parts of Deuteronomy 29 and 34. The essence of the law is in Deuteronomy 12-26 inclusive.

3

The Law of Holiness

Leviticus 17-26
Date about 600 B. C.
(Cited as H)

This code according to some writers was compiled by Ezekiel, though Driver [1] dissents from this view.

It contains but little civil or criminal law, but relates chiefly to moral and ceremonial law. It does contain,

[1] Driver's *Introduction to the Literature of the Old Testament,* page 148.

however, humane sentiments. It emphasizes the idea of sin in its personal aspect, whereas before sin had been regarded chiefly as social or tribal. In the earlier periods of Jewish history when a crime was committed the whole tribe must suffer and make expiation. This was the inevitable result of a state of society where the family was the unit, and where individuals were of value only as members of the family or tribe. The idea that sin was personal was a distinct advance on former theories. Its appeal to conscience is new in Jewish experience. The nearest approach perhaps in the whole Pentateuch to the lofty spiritual ideals of Jesus is found in Leviticus 19^{18}, "Thou shalt love thy neighbor as thyself."

That H constituted an independent code see Leviticus 26^{46}.

4

The Priestly Code

Date 444 B. C.

Ex. $25\text{-}31^{18a}$, 35-40
Leviticus 1-16. 27
Parts of Genesis and Numbers
(Cited as P)

The Priestly Code was no doubt compiled in its present form about 500 B. C. during and shortly after the Babylonian Captivity. It was read by Ezra to the people in 444 B. C., Neh. $12^{1\text{-}3}$, and marks definitely the transformation of the Jewish race into a Jewish church. The political independence of Israel had been utterly destroyed and her principal men had been in exile in Babylon for two generations. The old idea of temporal power had to be abandoned. In its place was developed the conception of the spiritual mission of the Jewish people. The Priestly Code was well adapted to foster this conception and to hasten the process of transformation.

The church must now have an elaborate ritual. The Temple at Jerusalem became the absolute center of Jewish religious life and its accompanying ceremonies. The rules for sacrifices, for tithes, the law of clean and unclean, the sacred dues, and various ceremonies to atone for the sins of the people, constitute the bulk of this code. Its minute regulations, however, of the daily life of the Hebrews tended to formalism and hypocrisy, which gradually hardened into mere ceremonialism in which morals were too often relegated to the background and conduct was obscured by ritual.

P was accepted as authoritative as early as 250 B. C. Some of P is pre-exilic in origin. Its elaboration came later in the great Code. Sometimes it contradicts D, usually it supplements it. Its purpose was to stamp individuality on the Jewish race and its religion. Hence the emphasis on sin, the need of purification. To accomplish the latter an elaborate ritual was devised. It was collected in small codes, and these compiled some time after Nehemiah.

A brief comparison of D and P will be found profitable.

D commands the establishment of a central sanctuary at Jerusalem.	P presupposes this sanctuary as already existing.
D states the priests belonged to the tribe of Levi and that all Levites exercised priestly functions.	P says they were of the family of Aaron and makes a sharp distinction between priests and Levites.
D prescribes three agricultural feasts.	P prescribes six.

D orders that the tithes for the priesthood shall be vegetables.	P orders they shall be of the flocks and herds.
	P has a loftier conception of the Deity. It describes the origins of Israel's institutions, some of which were unknown before the Exile, and which demonstrates that P also was unknown prior to that time.

5

Early Laws

Our study in the following pages embraces primarily only the statutes and codes gathered up into the Torah, at the time of the closing of the legal canon. Many references to the Law are found in the prophets and other parts of the Old Testament. These did not have the same binding force and did not command the reverence and respect which the Jews entertained for the Law itself. Wherever these statements of the law are of especial interest or importance they have been cited in their appropriate places. No attempt has been made, for the obvious reason above referred to, to include all the instances where laws have been cited or prescribed in the histories, prophecies, or wisdom writings of the Old Testament.

The foregoing codes do not by any means include all of Israel's laws. Scattered throughout the Pentateuch are many ordinances, either single or in small groups, which went to make up the Torah. These are included in our study but are difficult to classify and in most instances it is impossible to assign a true date or authorship. The internal evidence very often is all we have to go by. The practical difficulty in conforming to our plan of showing chronological development so far as may be done, is therefore apparent. When possible these are referred to their true place in the legal canon, by proper designation. In most instances no dating or other data can be furnished.

We have had to be content to designate those laws which can be traced back of the specific groups known as Codes, as Early Laws. Generally speaking, this means before 800 B. C., although many single laws were formulated, or at least written down and announced, at much later dates.

6

Code of Ezekiel

Ezekiel 40-48
Date 572 B. C.

This is a theoretical code formulated by the prophet Ezekiel 572 B. C., while in captivity in Babylon. It was never adopted by the Jews and its value is chiefly historical and illustrative. Coming as it did between D and P, it bridges the intellectual gulf between the two and furnishes us data as to the processes of legislation that were going on. For the reason that it was a paper code only, not regarded as binding in any legal sense, no extended analysis of it is attempted.

7

Later Laws

The Captivity in Babylon exercised a profound influence, not only over the Jewish national life, but their ways of thinking and individual modes of life. What more rational conclusion to the proud but tortured race than that they had incurred the deep displeasure of Yahweh? And, casting about for some means to regain his lost favor, what offered greater promise of success than strict observance of the rites which priests claimed Yahweh had commanded? A Sabbath devoted solely to worship, a Day of Atonement in which the national soul profoundly humbled itself, were fruits of the tragic experiences through which they had passed. The priestly laws reflect the great change in which sacrifice became central, instead of the lofty ethical exhortations of the prophets.

But even the code of 444 B. C. known as P did not answer all perplexing questions or accomplish the desired result. To meet new conditions new laws were adopted from time to time, were announced to the people, and in time took their place in the sacred volume of the Torah. By 250 B. C. most of the present Law was definitely compiled and accepted as authority. These later laws did not constitute any definite body of ordinances which could be called a code. They are cited, however, to show the latest development of that entire system of statutes, ordinances, decisions and judgments which collectively form the Torah, the great Law Book of Israel.

8

A general glance at these various codes and their chronology convinces us that the Law was much less ancient than has been popularly supposed. Instead of having its origin in Moses in 1300 B. C. only a law here and there of the most rudimentary type can be traced so far back. Some of them date as late as 250 B. C. The great bulk of them came into existence between 800 and 400 B. C., at least so far as their present written form is concerned. Without these facts constantly in mind no study of Old Testament Law can be accurate or complete.

9

Summary

By way of summary we may say that the Pentateuch is made up of (1) two streams of narrative or history, that in which the term Yahweh is used and hence is designated as J, and that in which Elohim is used, and known as E. These two accounts sometimes cover the same ground, and sometimes differ widely. Modern criticism has traced the passages belonging to each and arranged each in a continuous story. These were united by a later editor and are known among scholars as JE; and (2) the legal sections, or the Torah proper. The latter are nearly all found in Exodus 20-23, 25-31, 34-35; Leviticus 1-8, 11-25, 27; Numbers 5-10, 18, 19, 27-30; Deuteronomy 4 to 26. The bulk of the civil law is contained in Exodus 21-23 and Deuteronomy 21-25. The Law of Holiness, Leviticus 17-26, is interpolated in the Priestly Code, although clearly out of place there. Laws of Inheritance are chiefly in Numbers 27 and 36. The ceremonial law P in Exodus 25-31, 35-40; Leviticus 1-16, 27. The Decalogue is in JE. The "Words" are in Exodus 20^{23-26}, $22^{18-24. 28-31}$, 23^{1-19}, Judgments in Exodus 21^{1}, $22^{17. 25-27}$. C is older than E; and D is largely a repetition and expansion of the non-priestly parts of JE and is not possibly of Mosaic origin. (Jewish Cyc., Vol. 5, p. 542.) That the laws in JE, Exodus 20-23, are the foundation of the Deuteronomic legislation becomes certain. For example, Deuteronomy 17^{2-7} is an expansion of Exodus 22^{24}, Deuteronomy 16^{1-17}, of Exodus 23^{14-17}, and Deuteronomy $18^{10. 11}$, of Exodus 22^{18}. E dates from 900 to 750 B. C., J from 850 to 750 B. C.

OLD TESTAMENT LAW

Classification, Text and Explanatory Notes

ORIGIN OF ISRAEL'S LAWS

Historical Note

The uniform tradition of the Jews through their entire history ascribed the origin of their laws to their great lawgiver, Moses. Yahweh spake to his chosen people and Moses received the divine commands as their representative. Laws were therefore Yahweh's laws. If they were obeyed they brought his favor. If disobeyed his displeasure would be heavy upon them. Divine sanction gave these laws great authority. Without that sanction they would have counted but little.

In time all laws were referred back to Moses, although most of them were enacted centuries after his death. As time passed his name became the synonym of majesty, authority, divine favor. Statutes and ceremonies were ascribed to him although applying to facts and conditions that arose centuries later. Codes were accepted because stamped with his name. The tradition grew until nothing could shake the implicit faith of the Jews in their great teacher, judge and lawgiver.

The Torah was the divine message of Jehovah to Israel through Moses.

The laws of Israel were given through Moses by direct command of Jehovah.

(J)[1] Ex. 19[20] 20[1]
(E) 24[12] 32[15. 16. 19b.]
(D) Dt. 4[44. 45.] 5[1-5]
31[9-12. 24-26.]
32[46] 33[4]
(P) Ex. 31[18] 34[1-4. 29]
Jos. 1[8] 8[32-34]
23[6] 24[26]
Neh. 8[1-3]

These laws must be read to the people every seven years.

(D) Dt. 31[9-13]

And placed by the side of the Ark of the Covenant.

(D) Dt. 31[26]

There are wonderful promises to Israel if these laws are observed.

(D) Dt. 28[1-14]
(H) Lev. 26[3-12]

Fearful punishments are threatened for disobedience.

(D) Dt. 28[15-68]
(H) Lev. 26[14-39]

The Later Covenant.

Jer. 31[31-34]

[1] The letters J., E., etc., refer to the various codes or constituent elements of the Pentateuch as heretofore described.

NOTE:—It has been thought unnecessary to set out in full all the passages cited. The text is set out in sufficient instances to illustrate the various laws, leaving the student to refer to the Bible for the other passages cited. Citations are repeated under different headings where applicable. The text follows the citation to which it belongs.

PUBLIC LAW

A

CIVIL GOVERNMENT

I

KIND OF GOVERNMENT

1

Historical Note

1. *The Patriarchal Age.* In primitive times the family was the unit of Hebrew life. The conditions of living were so simple that no elaborate form of government was possible and but few laws were needed. The father as head of the family was the supreme ruler, with power of life and death in certain instances. The tribal form of government gradually grew out of this system and was fully developed at the time of the conquest of Canaan. The earliest laws make no reference to king, state, or judges.

2. *Government by Judges.* When the Jewish tribes were united together with some degree of solidarity, certain men by personal ascendancy acquired power over the scattered tribes. These men were called Judges. Their authority was based rather on voluntary submission than express sanction.

3. *The Monarchy.* The danger of invasion and overthrow by the Philistines resulted in the election of Saul as King. Under his immediate successors, David and Solomon, the fortunes of the Jews reached their highest point. With various vicissitudes the Kingdom survived until the Babylonian Captivity.

4. *Priestly Government.* After the exile the Jewish State was in fact transformed into a Jewish Church. It then became a genuine theocracy, with the priests as the actual rulers. The High Priest obtained great power and authority. This form of government continued with some intermissions until the conquest by the Romans.

It should be remembered that under all these various forms of government Jewish laws were largely of a religious nature, the difference between civil and religious laws as at present understood being practically unknown. There was no legislative body or authority. All laws were supposed to have been handed down by Jehovah and to have his divine sanction. The functions of government were mainly judicial and military, interpreting and enforcing the laws of Jehovah, and making war on Israel's enemies. There was very little of an administrative organization to enforce civil regulations, such as did exist relating chiefly to the collection of taxes for the support of the monarchy. The complex civil systems of modern states had not developed, trade and commerce were of a very simple nature, and there was but little communication between the tribes themselves or with other nations. This primitive state of society must be constantly kept in view in studying the government of Israel and its various laws.

2

The Rulers of Israel

(1) *Power of Father over children.*

(E) Gen. 22 38 [24]
Ju. 11 [30-31]

"And Jephthah vowed a vow unto Jehovah, and said, If thou wilt indeed deliver the children of Ammon into my hand, then it shall be, that whatsoever cometh forth from the doors of my house to meet me, when I return in peace from the children of Ammon, it shall be Jehovah's, and I will offer it up for a burnt offering."

This power was in certain cases limited.

(D) Dt. 21 [18-21]

The heads of families made covenants relative to settling disputes between their children and dependents.

(E) Gen. 21 [22-24]

(2) *The Elders of the city had certain authority.*

Ju. 8 [6. 14. 16.]

They might select their own successor in some cases.

Ju. 11 [5-6]

Women might have authority under the system of Judges.

Ju. 5 [12]

(3) *Hebrew Kings did not have autocratic power. The first King Saul was chosen by the people.*

1 Sam. 10 [24] 11 [14]

The people asked for a King when Saul was chosen.

1 Sam. 8 [4-5]

The King anointed.

1 Sam. 10 [1]

The King was a judge and military leader.

1 Sam. 8 [20]

The King as judge.

2 Sam. 15 [2]

The King made political alliances.

Is. 7 [1] 2 K. 16 [5]

He must be a Jew.

(D) Dt. 17 [14-15]

His power was limited.

(D) Dt. 17 [16.17]

1 K. 21ff.

Was chief religious head and adviser.

1 K. 12 [32-33]

2 K. 16 [12]

After the exile the Jews became a church, rather than a nation. Priests were the real rulers and the High Priests had supreme authority.

1 Mac. 12 [6] 14 [20]

3

Qualifications for Citizenship

By inference it would seem that all male Jews were entitled to citizenship. Exceptions were:—

(D) Dt. 23 [1. 2.]

Naturalization laws for foreigners were as follows:—

Ammonites and Moabites could never become citizens, at least to the tenth generation.

(E) Dt. 23 [3]

But Edomites and Egyptians of the third generation were permitted to become citizens.

(D) Dt. 23 [7. 8.]

4

Laws Relating to Aliens

Historical Note

Jewish laws relating to foreigners were strikingly humane for that period. In some respects they correspond to modern naturalization laws. Those who were permitted to enter and become citizens were treated with marked consideration. When it is remembered that among all Semitic tribes slavery was common, it is noteworthy that the Jews treated slaves as in some cases possible citizens. The lot of slaves was much better than in Rome or other ancient nations. It is true that captured men and women were treated as prizes of war, almost as booty. It is also true that men were sold as slaves for debt. But in this connection we must remember the custom of most civilized nations in modern times, where until a comparatively recent period poverty was considered a crime and men could be imprisoned indefinitely for debt. Indeed, imprisonment for debt survived long after many other barbarous customs had disappeared before an enlightened public conscience. The rights of property were more sacred than the rights of persons.

Jewish laws bear fair comparison in this respect with the laws of European countries as late as the seventeenth century.

Laws should apply equally to aliens.

(C) Ex. 22[21] 23[9]
12[49]

"One law shall be to him that is home-born, and unto the stranger that sojourneth among you."

(H) Lev. 19[34]

"The stranger that sojourneth with you shall be unto you as the home-born among you, and thou shalt love him as thyself; for ye were sojourners in the land of Egypt; I am Jehovah Your God."

(H) Lev. 24[22]

"Ye shall have one manner of law, as well for the sojourner, as for the home-born: for I am Jehovah your God."

(P) Nu. 9[14] 15[14-16] 35[15]
(D) Dt. 1[16] 24[14. 17. 18.] 27[19]

But in certain respects their rights were different.

A foreigner could not marry a Jew.

(P) Gen. 34[14]

Nor own slaves.

(H) Lev. 25[47-48]

Interest could be charged to a foreigner.

(D) Dt. 23[20]

"Unto a foreigner thou mayest lend upon interest; but unto thy brother thou shalt not lend upon interest; that Jehovah thy God may bless thee in all that thou puttest thy hand unto, in the land whither thou goest in to possess it."

The Sabbatical release of debts did not apply to foreigners.

(D) Dt. 15[2. 3.]

"And this is the manner of the release: Every creditor shall release that which he hath lent unto his neighbor; he shall not exact it of his neighbor, and his brother; because Jehovah's release hath been proclaimed.

"Of a foreigner thou mayest exact it: but whatsoever of thine is with thy brother thy hand shall release."

A dead animal might be sold to a foreigner.

(D) Dt. 14 [21]

5

Slaves and Slavery

Slavery was common from the earliest times. Slaves were taken captive in war, were bought, were inherited, or were taken for debt.

Slavery might be perpetual.

(C) Ex. 21 [5-7]

"But if the servant shall plainly say, I love my master, my wife, and my children; I will not go out free; then his master shall bring him unto God, and shall bring him to the door, or unto the door post; and his master shall bore his ear through with an awl; and he shall serve him for ever.

And if a man sell his daughter to be a maidservant, she shall not go out as the menservants do."

But only foreigners or resident aliens could be permanent bondmen.

(H) Lev. 25 [44-45]

Slaves were sometimes inherited.

Lev. 25 [46]

Were bought.

(C) Ex. 21 [2. 7.]
2 K. 4 [1]
Neh. 5 [5-8]
Jer. 34 [8]
Is. 50 [1. 2]
Job. 24 [9]

Or sold for debt.

Am. 2[6] 8[6]

(D) Dt. 15[12]

"If thy brother, a Hebrew man, or a Hebrew woman, be sold unto thee, and serve thee six years; then in the seventh year thou shalt let him go free from thee."

(H) Lev. 25[39]

Sold for theft.

(C) Ex. 22[3]

Jewish servants were to be released in the Sabbatical year.

(C) Ex. 21[2]

Women captives were treated as slaves.

Ju. 5[30]

"Have they not found, have they not divided the spoil? A damsel, two damsels to every man; to Sisera a spoil of dyed garments, a spoil of dyed garments embroidered, dyed garments embroidered on both sides, on the necks of the spoil?"

Or treated as booty.

(D) Dt. 20[14]

Slave regarded as his master's money.

(E) Ex. 20[17]
(J) Gen. 12[16]

And part of his master's household.

(E) Ex. 20[17]

Sometimes he was the special property of his mistress.

(J) Gen. 16[5a. 9.]
(P) 25[12]
(J) 30[3]
(J) 24[59]
(P) 29[24. 29.]

Maid servants regarded as concubines.

(C) Ex. 21[7-11]
(H) Lev. 19[20]

Servants could be flogged by master.

(C) Ex. 21[20] (D) Dt. 23[15]

If maimed by master were given freedom.

(C) Ex. 21 [26-27]

"And if a man smite the eye of his servant, or the eye of his maid, and destroy it; he shall let him go free for his eye's sake.

And if he smite out his manservant's tooth, or his maidservant's tooth; he shall let him go free for his tooth's sake."

Protection for captive wives.

(D) Dt. 21 [10-14]

Probably could not own property while a servant.

(D) Dt. 15 [12-13]

Injury to a servant punished by fine paid to master.

(C) Ex. 22 [16]
(D) Dt. 22 [28-29]

"If a man find a damsel that is a virgin, that is not betrothed, and lay hold on her, and lie with her, and they be found; then the man that lay with her shall give unto the damsel's father fifty shekels of silver, and she shall be his wife; because he hath humbled her; he may not put her away all his days."

Foreign servants to have same rights as Jewish.

(E) Gen. 15 [3] (P) 17 [12]

Murder of a slave punished by death.

(C) Ex. 21 [12]
(H) Lev. 24 [17]

A slave must be circumcised.

(P) Ex. 12 [44]
(P) Gen. 17 [12]

And may then eat holy things.

(H) Lev. 22 [10ff.]
(P) Ex. 12 [44]

Compensation for Damages to Slaves.

(C) 30 shekels—Ex. 21 [32]
(E) 20 " —Gen. 37 [28]

Number of slaves compared to freemen 1 to 6.

Neh. 7 [60ff.]

Redemption of Slaves and Servants.

(C) Ex. $21^{2.\ 3.\ 8.\ 9.}$

(D) Dt. 21^{10-17} 15^{12-18}

(H) Lev. $25^{10.\ 47-55}$

Return of fugitive servants forbidden.

(D) Dt. $23^{15.\ 16.}$

6

Inferior Officers

Heads of Tribes and Families.

(P) Nu. 1^{4}

"And with you there shall be a man of every tribe; every one head of his father's house."

Princes of tribes.

(P) Nu. 1^{44}

Minor Officers.

(D) Dt. 20^{9}

Appointment of 70.

(JE) Nu. 11^{16}

Taking the Census.

(P) Nu. 1^{1-3} $3^{5-10.\ 14.\ 15.}$ 4^{1-3} 26^{2}

This was of priestly origin and was introduced late in Jewish history. Among Semitic tribes there is even to-day an aversion to being numbered.

Priests as civil servants.

2 Sam. $20^{23ff.}$

Captain of the hosts.

2 Sam. 12^{27}

Leader of Mighty Men of Valor.

2 Sam. 8^{18} 20^{23}

Recorder, probably the chief minister.

2 Sam. 8^{16} 20^{24}

2 K. 18^{18}

2 Chr. 34^{8}

Scribe; probably the Secretary of State.

2 K. $18^{18.\ 37}$

Officer over the tribute—collector of taxes.
2 Sam. 20 [24]
Governor of Royal Household—High Chamberlain.
Is. 36 [3. 22] 22 [15]
King's Servant.
2 K. 22 [12]
King's friend.
1 K. 4 [5]
King's Counselor.
1 Ch. 27 [33]
Head of Wardrobe.
2 K. 22 [14]
Governor of City.
1 K. 22 [26]

7

Taxation

Administrative functions of Government being simple heavy taxes were not required.

Census taken for tax purposes. (See note on preceding page.)
2 S. 24 [1]
Division of land for purposes of taxation.
1 K. 4 [7]
Crown Lands.
Ezek. 45 [7. 8.] 48 [21]
1 Ch. 27 [25]
Am. 7 [1]
Forced labor as tax.
1 K. 5 [13]
Confiscation of property.
1 K. 21
Stripping the Temple.
2 K. 18 [15]

"And Hezekiah gave him all the silver that was found

in the house of Jehovah, and in the treasures of the king's house."

Sea Trade a royal Monopoly.

1 K. 10^{15}

Land Tax indicated.

1 S. $8^{14. 15}$

Land Tax.

2 K. 23^{35}

Personal property taxed one tenth.

1 S. $8^{15. 17}$

Tribute from foreign rulers and toll on trade caravans.

1 K. 10^{15}

B

MILITARY LAWS

(1) *Wars were wars of Jehovah.*

(JE) Nu. 21^{14}

Soldiers sanctified before going into battle.

Jos. 3^{5}

(2) *Age of Soldiers.*

(P) Nu. $1^{2. 3. 18b. 20. 45.}$

(P) $26^{2a. 4a.}$

(3) *Exemption from Military Service.*

(1) *Of individuals.*

(D) Dt. $20^{1a. 5\text{-}8}$

"When thou goest forth to battle against thine enemies, and seest horses, and chariots, and a people more than thou, thou shalt not be afraid of them:"

"And the officers shall speak unto the people, saying, What man is there that hath built a new house, and hath not dedicated it? let him go and return to his house, lest he die in the battle, and another man dedicate it.

And what man is there that hath planted a vineyard, and hath not used the fruit thereof? let him go and return unto his house, lest he die in the battle, and another man use the fruit thereof.

And what man is there that hath betrothed a wife, and hath not taken her? let him go and return unto his house, lest he die in the battle, and another man take her.

And the officers shall speak further unto the people, and they shall say, What man is there that is fearful and faint-hearted? let him go and return unto his house, lest his brethren's heart melt as his heart."

(D) Dt. 24 [5]

"When a man taketh a new wife, he shall not go out in the host, neither shall he be charged with any business; he shall be free at home one year, and shall cheer up his wife, whom he hath taken."

1 Mac. 3 [55]

(2) *Of Levites.*

(P) Nu. 1 [48. 49]

"For Jehovah spake unto Moses, saying,

Only the tribe of Levi thou shalt not number, neither shalt thou take the sum of them among the children of Israel:"

(P) Nu. 2 [33]

Selective Draft.

(P) Nu. 31 [3-6]

The foregoing clearly indicated provisions as to the care used in selecting soldiers similar to those in modern use known as the selective draft.

(3) *Cleanliness in Camp.*

(D) Dt. 23 [9-14]

(4) *Manner of Attack.* Notice to Enemy.

(D) Dt. 20 [1-4 10-12]

Sounding alarm.

(P) Nu. 10 [9]

Food trees spared.

(D) Dt. 20 [19. 20]

"When thou shalt besiege a city a long time, in making war against it to take it, thou shalt not destroy the trees thereof by wielding an axe against them; for thou mayest eat of them, and thou shalt not cut them down; for is the tree of the field man, that it should be besieged of thee?

Only the trees of which thou knowest that they are not trees for food, thou shalt destroy and cut them down; and thou shalt build bulwarks against the city that maketh war with thee, until it fall."

(5) *Captives.*

Women were spared if of a foreign nation.

(D) Dt. 21[10-14]

But if inhabitants of Canaan all captives were killed.

(D) Dt. 20[16. 17]

All persons destroyed.

(D) Dt. 2[34]

"And we took all his cities at that time, and utterly destroyed every inhabited city with the woman, and the little ones; we left none remaining."

(D) Dt. 3[6. 7.]
Jos. 11[14]

Only men killed.

(P) Nu. 31[7]

"And they warred against Midian, as Jehovah Commanded Moses; and they slew every male."

(D) Dt. 20[10. 12. 16. 17.]
7[1. 2. 16.]

Men and married women killed.

(P) Nu. 31[17. 18.]

"Now therefore kill every male among the little ones, and kill every woman that hath known man by lying with him.

But all the women-children, that have not known a man by lying with him, keep alive for yourselves."

Only virgins spared.

(P) Nu. 31[17. 18.]

The foregoing provisions have been universally condemned in modern times as indicating a barbarous state of society. Especially is this the case since the Jews claimed these acts were done by express command of Jehovah. It will be observed that these rules had their origin in the earliest law codes and hence relate back to a nomadic, semi-savage state of society, when the Jews were engaged in fierce warfare with the inhabitants of Canaan and were fighting for their very existence.

There is a plausible suggestion of another and cogent reason. It has been supposed that sexual diseases were common among the Midianites, and that this drastic command was executed to prevent the spread of these diseases among the Jews.

(6) *Booty.*

(P) Nu. 31 [21-31]
(D) Dt. 20 [14]
1 S. 30 [21-31]

One half of booty went to the soldiers.

(P) Nu. 31 [42]

One half to priests and Levites.

(P) Nu. 31 [29. 30.]

(7) *War Indemnity.*

2 K. 3 [4]

"Now Mesha king of Moab was a sheepmaster: and he rendered unto the king of Israel the wool of a hundred thousand lambs, and of a hundred thousand rams."

The belief that indiscriminate massacre was commanded by Jehovah was in accordance with the barbarous ideas and cruel customs of the time. Religious conceptions in such a state of society were on a par with their ideas of tribal and individual justice, which in turn are reflected in their courts and system of administering justice.

C

COURTS AND LEGAL PROCEDURE

COURTS

Explanatory Note

The development of a system of courts for the prompt and efficient administration of justice is an index to the civilization of a people. The more complex the conditions of life the more numerous are the instances of possible disputes between individuals. The first duty of a state is to require all persons who have grievances to submit them to an impartial tribunal which, to be effective, must be established and maintained by the state. The second duty is to compel obedience to the court's judgment and decrees when rendered. It is a difficult and delicate matter to ascertain what is right amid the most perplexing circumstances of ignorance, prejudice, actual fraud, and in many instances conflicting interests. How successfully this is done determines the degree of mental and moral development of a people and through that its progress as a civilized community.

Compared with their primitive political organizations and moral ideas the judicial system developed in ancient Jewish times seems to be fairly representative. They did not record their judicial degrees and hence these could serve only to a limited degree as precedents. There was at first no public authority to enforce the court's findings. This was largely left to their moral effect on the parties. There was no military power back of the court. They did have a rudimentary code of trials and rules for the admission of evidence, most of which commend themselves to us for their essential wisdom and justice.

The origin of a judicial and at the same time legislative system is seen in Exodus 18 [13-26]. There it is related that causes of dispute between individuals were brought to Moses in such numbers that he was unable to hear them all. So he appointed able men out of Israel who served as judges to decide all ordinary questions. We may see the rudiments of a Supreme Court in the fact that only the hard causes were heard by Moses, whose wisdom and authority commanded unquestioning obedience.

Compare the custom of Roman Emperors to sit in judgment in the porch of the imperial palace on the Palatine; the custom of English monarchs to entertain jurisdiction of cases where for some reason the strict rules of the law failed to render justice, which developed later, through experienced chancellors appointed to represent the king, into the splendid system of chancery jurisprudence which is now one of the chief glories of English and American law.

A court of law followed strict technical rules which must be observed regardless of the results in individual cases. Much injustice resulted. Exceptional cases, in which the miscarriage of justice was flagrant were appealed to the king. These were referred to an expert who applied equitable principles so far as possible, and this practice resulted in the development, outside of and parallel with the law courts of an entire body of rules designed to secure exact justice between litigants. The courts which apply these rules are courts of equity, or chancery.

It would be most interesting to compare the following rules taken from Jewish law with the parallel rules in our modern judicial systems. Occasional notes are given to suggest studies along these lines.

Compare for instance the appointment of judges as shown herein with their appointment or election in our American States. It may be noted that generally speaking, federal judges are appointed, and state judges elected.

A

APPOINTMENT OF JUDGES AND THEIR JURISDICTION

(E) Ex. 18 [13-26]

"And it came to pass on the morrow, that Moses sat to judge the people: and the people stood about Moses from the morning unto the evening.

And when Moses' father-in-law saw all that he did to the people, he said, What is this thing that thou doest to the people? why sittest thou thyself alone, and all the people stand about thee from morning unto even?

And Moses said unto his father-in-law, Because the people come unto me to inquire of God:

When they have a matter, they come unto me; and I judge between a man and his neighbor, and I make them know the statutes of God, and his laws.

And Moses' father-in-law said unto him, The thing that thou doest is not good.

Thou wilt surely wear away, both thou, and this people that is with thee: for the thing is too heavy for thee; thou art not able to perform it thyself alone.

Hearken now unto my voice, I will give thee counsel, and God be with thee: be thou for the people to God-ward, and bring thou the causes unto God:

And thou shalt teach them the statutes and the laws, and shalt show them the way wherein they must walk, and the work that they must do.

Moreover thou shalt provide out of all the people able men, such as fear God, men of truth, hating unjust gain; and place such over them, to be rulers of thousands, rulers of hundreds, rulers of fifties, and rulers of tens:

And let them judge the people at all seasons: and it shall be, that every great matter they shall bring unto thee, but every small matter they shall judge themselves: so shall it be easier for thyself, and they shall bear the burden with thee.

If thou shalt do this thing, and God command thee so, then thou shalt be able to endure, and all this people also shall go to their place in peace.

So Moses hearkened to the voice of his father-in-law, and did all that he had said.

And Moses chose able men out of all Israel, and made them heads over the people, rulers of thousands, rulers of hundreds, rulers of fifties, and rulers of tens.

And they judged the people at all seasons: the hard causes they brought unto Moses, but every small matter they judged themselves."

(D) Dt. 16 [18a]
(JE) Nu. 11 [16]
2 Ch. 19 [4-11]

"And Jehosaphat dwelt at Jerusalem: and he went out again among the people from Beer-sheba to the hill-country of Ephraim, and brought them back unto Jehovah, the God of their fathers.

And he set judges in the land throughout all the fortified cities of Judah, city by city.

And said to the judges, Consider what ye do: for ye judge not for man, but for Jehovah; and he is with you in the judgment.

Now therefore let the fear of Jehovah be upon you: take heed and do it: for there is no iniquity with Jehovah our God, nor respect of persons, nor taking of bribes.

Moreover in Jerusalem did Jehosaphat set of the Levites and the priests, and of the heads of the fathers' houses of Israel, for the judgment of Jehovah, and for controversies. And they returned to Jerusalem.

And he charged them, saying, Thus shall ye do in the fear of Jehovah, faithfully, and with a perfect heart.

And whensoever any controversy shall come to you from your brethren that dwell in their cities, between blood and blood, between law and commandment, statutes and ordinances, ye shall warn them, that they be not guilty towards Jehovah, and so wrath come upon you and upon your brethren: this do, and ye shall not be guilty.

And, behold, Amariah the chief priest is over you in all matters of Jehovah; and Zebadiah the son of Ishmael, the ruler of the house of Judah, in all the king's matters; also the Levites shall be officers before you. Deal courageously, and Jehovah be with the good."

Appointment of vice judges.

(E) Ex. 24 [14]

A full judicial system is now in force.

(D) Dt. 19 [15-19]

"One witness shall not rise up against a man for any iniquity, or for any sin, in any sin that he sinneth; at the mouth of two witnesses, or at the mouth of three witnesses, shall a matter be established.

If an unrighteous witness rise up against any man to testify against him of wrong-doing, then both the men, between whom the controversy is, shall stand before Jehovah before the priests and the judges, that shall be in those days:

And the judges shall make diligent inquisition: and behold, if the witness be a false witness, and have testified falsely against his brother, then shall ye do unto him, as he had thought to do unto his brother: so shalt thou put the evil away from the midst of thee."

Submission of cases.

(C) Ex. 22 [8. 9.]

Moses was the earliest judge.

(E) Ex. 18 [13-27]

In small matters the priests were the judges.

(E) Ex. 18 [22]

The system of judges still in force at the time of Ezra.

Ezr. 7 [25] 10 [14]

"And thou, Ezra, after the wisdom of thy God that is in thine hand, appoint magistrates and judges, who may judge all the people that are beyond the River, all such as know the laws of thy God; and teach ye him that knoweth them not."

The King as judge.

At first the King heard only appeals. Afterward all important matters.

1 K. 3 [9]

"Give thy servant therefore an understanding heart to judge thy people, that I may discern between good and evil; for who is able to judge this thy great people?"

1 K. 7 [7]

"And he made a porch of the throne where he was to judge, even the porch of judgment: and it was covered with cedar from floor to floor."

2 K. 15 [5]
1 S. 8 [20]
2 S. 14 [4]
Am. 2 [3]
Hos. 7 [7]
Ps. 2 [10]

All ordinary cases of dispute were submitted to the judges for decision.

(D) Dt. 25 [1. 2.]

Exceptional cases were taken to the sanctuary, when the decisions were "decisions of Jehovah."

(C) Ex. 21 [6] 22 [7. 8]

The following special cases are noted.

Charges of unchastity against wife.

(D) Dt. 22 [15-21]
(P) Nu. 5 [12-31]

Where a person was accused of false witness.

(D) Dt. 19 [17-19]

Where a man was found slain in a field.

(D) Dt. 21 [1-9]

Judges must judge righteously.

(C) Ex. 23 [6-8]

"Thou shalt not wrest the justice due to thy poor in his cause.

Keep thee far from a false matter; and the innocent and righteous slay thou not: for I will not justify the wicked.

And thou shalt take no bribe: for a bribe blindeth them that have sight, and perverteth the words of the righteous."

(H) Lev. 19 [15] 24 [22]
(D) Dt. 16 [18-20]
25 [1. 2.]
1 [16. 17.]
(D) 27 [25]

These constant injunctions reveal the existence in Jewish society of both rich and poor, and the necessity of giving religious sanction to commands to render exact justice between the two classes. They are like a flash-light into ancient Jewish life, revealing clearly the division of society into classes and the difficulty then as now, of obtaining justice.

B

COURTS

Originally in Eastern lands there was no seperate Judiciary as in modern times. Those who decided disputes in fact exercised both judicial and legislative functions.

There soon arose the necessity to set apart certain persons whose sole duty was to determine causes in dispute. Later the division of function proceeded until civil suits were in general decided by judges, ethical questions by the prophets, ritual by the priests.

Courts were usually held at the city gates.

(D) Dt. 21 [19] 22 [15] 25 [7]

"Then shall his father and his mother lay hold on him, and bring him out unto the elders of his city, and unto the gate of his place."

Am. 5 [12. 15.]
Zech. 8 [16]

Sometimes in the Porch of Judgment.

1 K. 7 [7]

"And he made the porch of the throne where he was to judge, even the porch of judgment; and it was covered with cedar from floor to floor."

Origin of the Supreme Court.

(E) Ex. 18 [26.]

C

TRIALS

1. *Court Procedure.*

Parties brought their complaints to the judges after notice to the opposite party. Usually the statements of the parties were oral. Sometimes the complaint was written.

Job. 31 [35]

"Oh, that I had one to hear me! (Lo, here is my signature, let the Almighty answer me), and that I had the indictment which mine adversary hath written."

Judgment could be rendered on confession.

(P) Nu. 5 [6. 7.]

"Speak unto the children of Israel, When a man or woman shall commit any sin that men commit, so as to trespass against Jehovah, and that soul shall be guilty: then he shall confess his sin which he has done: and he shall make restitution for his guilt in full, and add unto it the fifth part thereof, and give it unto him in respect of whom he hath been guilty."

Otherwise witnesses were heard. The litigants brought their own witnesses.

In some cases a sort of trial by jury was had.

Talmud.

Contempt of court punished.

(C) Ex. 22 [28]

(D) Dt. 17 [12. 13.]

"And the man that doeth presumptuously, in not hearkening unto the priest that standeth to minister there before Jehovah thy God, or unto the judge, even that man shall die; and thou shalt put away the evil from Israel.

And all the people shall hear, and fear, and do no more presumptuously."

In cases of manslaughter there was a preliminary trial, similar to preliminary trials upon information in our modern practice, to determine probable guilt.

Jos. 20[4]

"And he shall flee unto one of those cities, and shall stand at the entrance of the gate of the city, and declare his cause in the ears of the elders of that city; and they shall take him into the city unto them, and give him a place, that he may dwell among them."

Final trial was had and judgment rendered by the "Congregation."

Jos. 20[5. 6.]

"And if the avenger of blood pursue after him, then they shall not deliver up the man-slayer into his hand; because he smote his neighbor unawares and hated him not beforetime.

And he shall dwell in that city, until he stand before the congregation for judgment, until the death of the high priest that shall be in those days: then shall the man-slayer return, and come unto his own city, and unto his own house, unto the city from whence he fled."

In modern practice when a man is arrested charged with a crime he must be taken forthwith before a Magistrate, usually a Justice of the Peace, for a preliminary trial. At this hearing he is entitled to counsel, as he is at all subsequent stages of the case. If the Magistrate finds no probable guilt the party is discharged. But if probable guilt is shown he is bound over to await the action of the next Grand Jury. There must be an indictment found before he can be tried. This method of procedure has been in force for centuries and was adopted to prevent the trial of innocent perons on groundless charges. Note the parallel procedure in primitive form among the Jews.

2. *Witnesses and Evidence.*

Witnesses must be of age and citizens. Slaves could not be witnesses.

The witnesses must take an oath before testifying.

(C) Ex. 22[10. 11]

"If a man deliver unto his neighbor an ass, or an ox, or a sheep, or any beast, to keep; and it die, or be hurt, or driven away no man seeing it: the oath of Jehovah shall be between them both, whether he hath not put his hand unto his neighbor's goods; and the owner thereof shall accept it, and he shall not make restitution."

For form of oaths see

(J) Gen. 31[50. 53.]
1 K. 2[23]
Ju. 8[19]
Jer. 42[5]

An oath was a conditional curse. Penalty for breaking.

(P) Lev. 6[1-7]

A witness must testify.

(P) Lev. 5[1]

Hearsay testimony not admitted.

Talmud.

Two witnesses required in cases of murder.

(P) Nu. 35[30]

"Whoso killeth any person, the murderer shall be slain at the mouth of witnesses: but one witness shall not testify against any person that die."

(D) Dt. 17[6. 7.]
(D) Dt. 19[15]

For certain purposes.

Ruth 4[11]

Duties of Witnesses.

(C) Ex. 23 [1-3]
(H) Lev. 19 [16]
(D) Dt. 17 [7]

To cast the first stone on infliction of death penalty.

Perjury punished.

(E) Ex. 20 [16]

"Thou shalt not bear false witness against thy neighbor."

(C) Ex. 23 [1]
(D) Dt. 5 [20]
19 [16-21]
(H) Lev. 19 [12]

D

JUDGMENTS

Judgments of the court were regarded as "Judgments of God."

(C) Ex. 22 [8. 9.]
(D) Dt. 1 [17]

"Ye shall not respect persons in judgment; ye shall hear the small and the great alike; ye shall not be afraid of the face of man; for the judgment is God's: and the cause that is too hard for you, ye shall bring unto me, and I will hear it."

Decisions were oral. In important cases they were preserved for precedents. There thus grew up a large body of law consisting of interpretations of the law by the various courts.

Judgments were rendered by the judges.

(D) Dt. 25 [1]

"If there be a controversy between men, and they come unto judgment, and the judges judge them; then they shall justify the righteous, and condemn the wicked."

Judgments were of two kinds.

1. Judgments in money.

These provided for restoration of property, or damages in money as the case required.

2. Judgments in Souls.

These worked corruption of blood, that is, loss of personal standing in the tribe, and loss of property and inheritance, or personal punishment.

These provisions are paralleled in modern times by similar rules, although corruption of blood and bills of attainder are unlawful in America.

Execution of Judgments

The whole power of the state is back of the decrees of the courts in modern nations. This gives them authority and compels respect and obedience.

In criminal cases sentences were enforced by the judges.

(D) Dt. 25 [2, 3]

"And it shall be, if the wicked man be worthy to be beaten, that the judge shall cause him to lie down, and to be beaten before his face, according to his wickedness, by number.

Forty stripes he may give him, he shall not exceed; lest, if he should exceed, and beat him above these with many stripes, then thy brother should seem vile unto thee."

In the execution of the death sentence the prosecuting witness must cast the first stone.

(D) Dt. 17 [7]

Relatives not to be punished.

(D) Dt. 24 [16]

This rule was established to correct a common custom in the East. For a precedent see

2 K. 14^{6}

E

APPEALS

It has always been regarded as necessary to allow appeals from the decisions of trial courts. Mistakes are often made in the trial of cases and not to provide for appeals would in many instances amount to a denial of justice. Appellate courts are universal in civilized communities. Made up of the abler and more experienced members of the bar, they are to a large extent removed from the influence of passion and prejudice. A study of the primitive system of appeals as used by the Jews is of great historical interest.

(1) The first appeals were to Moses.

(D) Dt. 1^{17} (E) Ex. 18^{26}

"Ye shall not respect persons in judgment; but ye shall hear the small as well as the great; ye shall not be afraid of the face of man; for the judgment is God's; and the cause that is too hard for you, bring it unto me, and I will hear it." (Moses speaking to the Israelites.)

(E) Ex. 18^{26b}

(2) Afterward to the priests.

(D) Dt. 17^{8-11}

"If there arise a matter too hard for thee in judgment, between blood and blood, between plea and plea, and between stroke and stroke, being matters of controversy within thy gates; then shalt thou arise, and get thee up into the place which Jehovah thy God shall choose: and thou shalt come unto the priests the Levites, and unto the judge that shall be in those days; and thou shalt inquire; and they shall shew thee the sentence of judgment:

And thou shalt do according to the tenor of the sentence, which they shall show thee from that place which

Jehovah shall choose; and thou shalt observe to do according to all that they shall teach thee: according to the tenor of the law which they shall teach thee, and according to the judgment which they shall tell thee, thou shalt do: thou shalt not turn aside from the sentence which they shall shew thee, to the right hand, nor to the left."

(D) Dt. 19 [17]

(3) To the King.

2 S. 14 [4-11]

1 K. 3 [16]

"Then came there two women that were harlots, unto the king, and stood before him."

(4) In the time of Christ to the Sanhedrin.

F

LAWYERS

There were no lawyers in early times. These came later with the multiplication of laws and especially the elaborate ceremonial provided for in the Priestly Code. The requirements of this Code were so complex and difficult to follow that numerous disputes resulted as to their proper observance. To decide these disputes and interpret the various provisions of the ritual there gradually grew up a body of learned men who were called Scribes. These corresponded to the lawyers of our day, only their duties were chiefly confined to giving rulings on or interpretations of religious statutes.

They received no pay, but became proud of their learning and exceedingly vain. Their decisions were authoritative when matters of the Law, or Torah were involved. In the time of Christ noted lawyers or scribes became members of the Sanhedrin, as, for instance, Hillel and Shammai, the leaders of the two leading Jewish schools of interpretation.

Also Gamaliel Ac. 5.
And Nicodemus Jn. 3 and 7.

G

INSTRUCTION IN THE LAW

Publishing the Law.

(D) Dt. 27 1-4

"And Moses and the elders of Israel commanded the people, saying, Keep all the commandment which I command you this day.

And it shall be on the day when ye shall pass over Jordan unto the land which Jehovah thy God giveth thee, that thou shalt set thee up great stones, and plaster them with plaster: and thou shalt write upon them all the words of this law, when thou art passed over; that thou mayest go in unto the land which Jehovah thy God giveth thee, a land flowing with milk and honey, as Jehovah, the God of thy fathers, hath promised thee.

And it shall be when ye are passed over the Jordan, that ye shall set up these stones, which I command you this day, in mount Ebal, and thou shalt plaster them with plaster."

(D) Dt. 27 8 31 9-13
Jos. 8 30-32
2 K. 23 1-3

"And the king sent, and they gathered unto him all the elders of Judah and of Jerusalem.

And the king went up to the house of Jehovah, and all the men of Judah and all the inhabitants of Jerusalem with him, and the priests, and the prophets, and all the people, both small and great; and he read in their ears all the words of the book of the covenant which was found in the house of Jehovah.

And the king stood by the pillar, and made a covenant before Jehovah, to walk after Jehovah, and to keep his commandments, and his testimonies, and his statutes, with all his heart and all his soul, to confirm the words of this covenant that were written in this book; and all the people stood to the covenant."

This undoubtedly relates to the Deuteronomic Law—discovered in the Temple 621 B. C.

The following relates to the Levitical or Priestly law—read by Ezra to the people 444 B. C. It is important as being the origin of P. Neh. 8 1-18

"And all the people gathered themselves together as one man into the broad place that was before the water gate; and they spake unto Ezra the scribe to bring the Book of the law of Moses, which Jehovah had commanded to Israel.

And Ezra the priest brought the law before the assembly, both men and women, and all that could hear with understanding, upon the first day of the seventh month.

And he read therein before the broad place that was before the water gate from early morning until midday, in the presence of the men and the women, and of those that could understand; and the ears of all the people were attentive unto the book of the law.

And Ezra the scribe stood upon a pulpit of wood, which they had made for the purpose; and beside him stood Mattithiah, and Shema, and Anaiah, and Uriah, and Hilkiah, and Maaseiah, on his right hand; and on his left hand, Pedaiah, and Mishael, and Malchiah, and Hashum, and Hashbadanah, Zechariah, and Meshullam.

And Ezra opened the book in the sight of all the people: (for he was above all the people;) and when he opened it, all the people stood up:

And Ezra blessed Jehovah, the great God. And all the people answered, Amen, Amen, with the lifting up of their hands: and they bowed their heads, and worshiped Jehovah with their faces to the ground.

Also Jeshua, and Bani, and Sherebiah, Jamin, Akkub, Shabbethai, Hodiah, Maaseiah, Kelita, Azariah Jozabad,

Hanan, Pelaiah, and the Levites, caused the people to understand the law: and the people stood in their place.

And they read in the book, in the law of God, distinctly; and gave the sense, so that they understood the reading.

And Nehemiah, who was the governor, and Ezra the priest the scribe, and the Levites that taught the people, said unto all the people, This day is holy unto Jehovah your God; mourn not, nor weep. For all the people wept, when they heard the words of the law.

Then he said unto them, Go your way, eat the fat, and drink the sweet, and send portions unto him for whom nothing is prepared; for this day is holy unto our Lord: neither be ye grieved: for the joy of Jehovah is your strength.

So the Levites stilled all the people, saying, Hold your peace, for the day is holy; neither be ye grieved.

And all the people went their way to eat, and to drink, and to send portions, and to make great mirth, because they had understood the words that were declared unto them.

And on the second day were gathered together the heads of the fathers' houses of all the people, the priests, and the Levites, unto Ezra the scribe, even to give attention to the words of the law.

And they found written in the law how that Jehovah had commanded by Moses, that the children of Israel should dwell in booths in the feast of the seventh month: and that they should publish and proclaim in all their cities, and in Jerusalem, saying, Go forth unto the mount, and fetch olive branches, and branches of wild olives, and myrtle branches, and palm branches, and branches of thick trees, to make booths, as it is written.

So the people went forth, and brought them, and made themselves booths, every one upon the roof of his house, and in their courts, and in the courts of the house of God, and in the broad place of the water gate, and in the broad place of the gate of Ephraim.

And all the assembly of them that were come again out of the captivity made booths, and dwelt in the booths; for since the days of Jeshua the son of Nun unto that day had not the children of Israel done so. And there was very great gladness.

Also day by day, from the first day unto the last day, he read in the book of the law of God. And they kept the feast seven days: and on the eighth day was a solemn assembly, according unto ordinances."

The Law shall be taught to children.

(D) Dt. 6[6-9 20-25] 11[18-21]

Preserve the Law without adding to or subtracting from.

(D) Dt. 4[2]

Study the Law.

(D) Dt. 6[6-7] 11[18-19]

H

DAMAGES FOR WRONGS AND BREACHES OF CONTRACT

Originally the lex talionis, or law of like for like was the only one recognized, as may well be imagined in a primitive state of society. Gradually there grew up a milder system, under which money compensation could be made in certain cases for wrongs committed or for breach of contract. This section does not include penalties for crimes, which will be included under the heading—Criminal Law.

The development of a graduated system of money compensations or damages to be substituted for former penalties marks a decided advance in primitive ideas of justice and its administration.

Damages

For maiming person.

(H) Lev. 24 [19]

"And if a man cause a blemish in his neighbor; as he hath done, so shall it be done to him;"

For stealing.

(C) Ex. 22 [1-5]

(P) 6 [2-7]

For kindling fire which damages property.

(C) Ex. 22 [6]

"If fire break out, and catch in thorns, so that the shocks of grain or the standing grain, or the field, are consumed he that kindled the fire shall surely make restitution."

For Breach of Trust, dealing and swearing falsely, robbery and oppression of neighbor.

(P) Lev. 6 [1-5]

"And Jehovah spake unto Moses, saying,

If any one sin, and commit a trespass against Jehovah, and deal falsely with his neighbor in a matter of deposit, or of bargain or of robbery, or have oppressed his neighbor, or have found that which was lost, and deal falsely therein, and swear to a lie; in any of all these things that a man doeth, sinning therein; then it shall be if he hath sinned, and is guilty, that he shall restore that which he took by robbery, or the thing which he hath gotten by oppression, or the deposit which was committed to him or the lost thing which he found, or anything about which he hath sworn falsely; he shall even restore it in full, and shall add the fifty part more thereto; unto him to whom it appertaineth shall he give it, in the day of his being found guilty."

For killing animal.

(P) Lev. 24 [18. 21]

Animal killing another animal.

(C) Ex. 21 [35. 36]

For stolen bailment.

(C) Ex. 22^{12}

For loss of animal falling into a pit.

(E) Ex. 21$^{33, 34}$

For loss of borrowed property.

(C) Ex. 22^{14}

What are known as punitive damages in modern law were allowed in certain cases, as penalties.

Double damages

For stealing.

(C) Ex. 22^{4}

"If the theft be found in his hand alive, whether it be ox, or ass, or sheep; he shall pay double."

For trespass by animals.

(C) Ex. 22^{5}

20% penalty.

For breach of trust, etc.

(P) Lev. 6$^{1\text{-}5}$

For various wrongs committed.

(P) Nu. 5$^{6\text{-}8}$

PRIVATE LAW

A

CIVIL LAW

1

Domestic Relations

1. *Marriage. Husband and Wife. Divorce*

The family was the unit of Jewish society. This included not only parents and children, but married children living with their parents, grandchildren, concubines and their children, servants and their children.

1

The marriage relation was recognized from the earliest times

(J) Gen. 2 [18]

"And Jehovah God said, It is not good that the man should be alone; I will make him a help meet for him."

(J) Gen. 2 [21-24]

"And Jehovah God caused a deep sleep to fall upon the man, and he slept; and he took one of his ribs, and closed up the flesh instead thereof; and the rib, which Jehovah God had taken from the man, made he a woman, and brought her unto the man.

And the man said, This is now bone of my bones, and flesh of my flesh; she shall be called Woman, because she was taken out of man.

Therefore shall a man leave his father and his mother, and shall cleave unto his wife: and they shall be one flesh."

(P) Nu. $30^{6\text{-}8\ 13.15.}$
(J) Gen. 16
(E) Gen. 29^{23}

Marriage with captive women permitted.

(D) Dt. $21^{10\text{-}13}$

"When thou goest forth to battle against thine enemies, and Jehovah thy God delivereth them into thine hands, and thou carriest them away captive, and seest among the captives a beautiful woman, and thou hast a desire unto her, and wouldest take her to thee to wife; then thou shalt bring her home to thy house; and she shall shave her head, and pare her nails; and she shall put the raiment of her captivity from off her, and shall remain in thy house, and bewail her father and her mother a full month: and after that thou shalt go in unto her, and be her husband, and she shall be thy wife."

Women must marry within the tribe.

(P) Nu. 36^{6}

After Seduction.

(C) Ex. 22^{16}
(D) Dt. $22^{28.\ 29}$

Slave could marry master's daughter.

1 Chr. $2^{34.\ 35.}$

"Now Sheshan had no sons, but daughters. And Sheshan had a servant, an Egyptian, whose name was Jarha.

And Sheshan gave his daughter to Jarha his servant to wife; and she bare him Attai."

2

Polygamy was common

(J) Gen. 4^{19}

"And Lamech took unto him two wives: the name of the one was Adah, and the name of the other Zillah."

1 Ch. 7^{4}

But the High Priest could have only one wife.

(H) Lev. 21 [13]

"And he shall take a wife in her virginity."

Several wives were forbidden kings.

(D) Dt. 17 [17]

Polygamy continued as late as New Testament times.

Priests could marry only a virgin.

(H) Lev. 21 [13-14]

The Levirate Law—to marry brother's widow.

(D) Dt. 25 [5-10]

"If brethren dwell together, and one of them die, and have no son, the wife of the dead shall not be married without unto a stranger: her husband's brother shall go in unto her, and take her to him to wife, and perform the duty of a husband's brother unto her.

And it shall be, that the firstborn which she beareth shall succeed in the name of his brother, that is dead, that his name be not blotted out of Israel.

And if the man like not to take his brother's wife, then his brother's wife shall go up to the gate unto the elders, and say, My husband's brother refuseth to raise up unto his brother a name in Israel; he will not perform the duty of my husband's brother unto me.

Then the elders of his city shall call him, and speak unto him: and if he stand, and say, I like not to take her; then shall his brother's wife come unto him in the presence of the elders, and loose his shoe from off his foot, and spit in his face: and she shall answer and say, So shall it be done unto the man that doth not build up his brother's house.

And his name shall be called in Israel, The house of him that hath his shoe loosed."

The purpose of this law is evident—to preserve the family, the unit of Jewish life.

3

Marriage forbidden

1. *As to relationship.*

(D) Dt. 22 [30]

"A man shall not take his father's wife, and shall not uncover his father's skirt."

(D) Dt. 27 [20. 22. 23.]
(H) Lev. 18 [6. 18.]
20 [11 12. 14. 17. 20. 21.]

Yet Abraham married his half sister.

(E) Gen. 20 [12]

2. *With Aliens.*

(D) Dt. 7 [1-3]
(P) Ex. 34 [12a. 15. 16.]
(P) Nu. 25 [6-8]
Neh. 13 [23-27]

In earlier times such marriages were not forbidden. Both David and Solomon had foreign wives—The purpose of the later prohibition was no doubt to preserve the racial identity.

3. *Priests.*

(H) Lev. 21 [7. 13-15.]

The wife under the Hebrew law became virtually the property of her husband. She had no legal redress if wronged by her husband.

(D) Dt. 5 [21a.]

"Neither shalt thou covet thy neighbor's wife; neither shall thou covet thy neighbor's house."

(E) Ex. 20 [17b.]

But practically wives were given much liberty and in numerous instances exercised great influence.

Divorce

Divorce was recognized, but was allowed only to the husband.

(H) Lev. 21[14] 22[13]
(C) Ex. 21[7-11]
(D) Dt. 21[10-14]
Dt. 24[1-4]

"When a man taketh a wife, and marrieth her, then it shall be, if she find no favor in his eyes, because he hath found some unseemly thing in her, then he shall write her a bill of divorcement, and give it in her hand, and send her out of his house.

And when she is departed out of his house, she may go and be another man's wife.

And if the latter husband hate her, and write her a bill of divorcement, and give it in her hand, and send her out of his house; or if the latter husband die, who took her to be his wife; her former husband, who sent her away, may not take her again to be his wife, after that she is defiled; for that is abomination before Jehovah: and thou shalt not cause the land to sin, which Jehovah thy God giveth thee for an inheritance."

The purpose was no doubt to make divorce somewhat difficult by requiring written reasons.

(P) Nu. 30[9]
Jer. 3[8]
Is. 50[1]

In case of seduction the husband could not divorce the wife.

(D) Dt. 22[28. 29.]

2. *Parent and Child*

(1) The father's power over his children was absolute, even extending to the death penalty.

Ju. 11[39]

"And it came to pass at the end of two months, that she returned unto her father, who did with her according to his vow which he had vowed: and she knew not man. And it was a custom in Israel."

He could sell a daughter into slavery.

(C) Ex. 21 [7]

"And if a man sell his daughter to be a maidservant, she shall not go out as the menservants do."

(P) Nu. 30 [3-5]

"Also when a woman voweth a vow unto Jehovah, and bindeth herself by a bond, being in her father's house, in her youth, and her father heareth her vow, and her bond wherewith she hath bound her soul, and her father holdeth his peace at her; then all her vows shall stand, and every bond wherewith she hath bound her soul shall stand.

But if her father disallow her in the day that he heareth, none of her vows, or of her bonds wherewith she hath bound her soul, shall stand: and Jehovah will forgive her, because her father disallowed her."

He could arrange for the marriage of his sons.

(J) Gen. 24 [4]

"But thou shalt go unto my country, and to my kindred, and take a wife for my son Isaac."

(P) Gen. 28 [2]

Ju. 14 [2]

(2) Honor due to parents.

(C) Ex. 20 [12]

"Honor thy father and thy mother, that thy days may be long in the land which Jehovah thy God giveth thee."

(D) Dt. 5 [16]

21 [18-21] 27 [16]

(C) Ex. 21 [15. 17]

(H) Lev. 19 [3] 20 [9]

3. *Master and Servant*

Servants bought.

(C) Ex. 21 [2-4]

"If thou buy a Hebrew servant, six years he shall serve; and in the seventh he shall go out free for nothing.

If he come in by himself, he shall go out by himself; if he be married, then his wife shall go out with him.

If his master give him a wife, and she bear his sons or daughters; the wife and her children shall be her master's, and he shall go out by himself."

(C) Ex. 21[7. 8.]

If Jews were slaves they were to be redeemed.

(H) Lev. 25[39-55]

Redemption of.

(C) Ex. 21[7-8]

"And if a man sell his daughter to be a maidservant, she shall not go out as the menservants do.

If she please not her master, who hath espoused her to himself, then shall he let her be redeemed: to sell her unto foreign people he shall have no power, seeing he hath dealt deceitfully with her."

(E) Ex. 21[26. 27]

Freeing of in Sabbatical Year. It will be noted this applies to Hebrew slaves, not to foreigners.

(C) Ex. 21[z-6]

(D) Dt. 15[12-18]

"If thy brother, a Hebrew man, or a Hebrew woman, be sold unto thee, and serve thee six years; then in the seventh year thou shalt let him go free from thee.

And when thou lettest him go free from thee, thou shalt not let him go empty: thou shalt furnish him liberally out of thy flock, and out of thy threshing floor, and out of thy winepress; as Jehovah thy God hath blessed thee thou shalt give unto him.

And thou shalt remember that thou wast a bondman in the land of Egypt, and Jehovah thy God redeemed thee: therefore I command thee this thing to-day.

And it shall be, if he say unto thee, I will not go away from thee; because he loveth thee and thy house, because he is well with thee; then thou shalt take an awl, and thrust it through his ear unto the door, and he shall be thy servant for ever. And also unto thy maidservant thou shalt do likewise.

It shall not seem hard unto thee, when thou lettest him go free from thee; for to the double of the hire of a hireling hath he served thee six years: and Jehovah thy God shall bless thee in all that thou doest."

Jer. 34 [8-16]

In the year of Jubilee.

(P) Lev. 25 [10. 54.]

The provisions for freeing slaves every seven years apparently contradicts these rules for freeing them in the year of Jubilee. It may be the former could not be enforced and the greater period was adopted to soften down the rule. Even then it was not strictly observed.

Injuries to slaves punished.

(C) Ex. 21 [20. 21. 26. 27. 32.]

"And if a man smite his servant, or his maid, with a rod, and he die under his hand; he shall surely be punished.

Notwithstanding, if he continue a day or two, he shall not be punished; for he is his money.

And if a man smite the eye of his servant, or the eye of his maid, and destroy it; he shall let him go free for his eye's sake.

And if he smite out his manservant's tooth, or his maidservant's tooth; he shall let him go free for his tooth's sake.

If the ox gore a manservant or a maidservant, there shall be given unto their master thirty shekels of silver, and the ox shall be stoned."

Wages of.

(H) Lev. 19 [13b]

(D) Dt. 24 [14. 15]

"Thou shalt not oppress a hired servant that is poor and needy, whether he be of thy brethren, or of thy sojourners that are in thy land within thy gates: in his day thou shalt give him his hire, neither shall the sun go down upon it; (for he is poor, and setteth his heart upon it;) lest he cry against thee unto Jehovah, and it be sin unto thee."

Religious rights.

(P) Ex. 12 [43. 44]
(D) Dt. 12 [17. 18]
16 [10. 11]
(H) Lev. 22 [10b]
25 [6]

Fugitive Slaves. Not returned.

(D) Dt. 23 [15. 16]

"Thou shalt not deliver unto his master a servant that is escaped from his master unto thee: he shall dwell with thee, in the midst of thee, in the place which he shall choose within one of thy gates, where it pleaseth him best: thou shalt not oppress him."

2

Laws of Inheritance

Historical Note

The laws relating to the descent of property upon the death of the owner have varied widely in different nations and periods of the world's history. The question was not important among primitive peoples where accumulations of property were small. But as men acquired fixed abodes and stable political conditions enabled them to amass property it was inevitable the question should assume importance. Where community rights were held paramount to the rights of individuals, as in a tribal stage of development, the individual could not alienate his property from the family or tribe. To do so would imperil the tribal life. There were therefore rules against selling land in perpetuity or willing it out of the tribe. Most ancient peoples had laws requiring the periodical redistribution of land. The early laws of the Jews contained these provisions, evidently designed to keep all property within the respective tribes and their constituent families. It served the purpose fairly well, although it was not thoroughly enforced and was often evaded.

In later ages the Jews became individualists as to property, stoutly claiming for each man the right to do as he pleased with his own.

In a more complex society social questions and considerations began to assert themselves. In many nations it has been observed that parents were disposed to leave their property to the oldest son or to a favorite child, thus tending to build up vast estates, the existence of which affected the well being of the community. The balance between the individual right of disposition and social control varies according to the numbers of inhabitants in a country, their wealth, industries, economic organization and stage of development.

In countries where a landed aristocracy is regarded as the foundation of national strength and security, primogeniture is adopted to secure this end as in England. Where a general diffusion of wealth among small landowners is deemed of vital importance, as in France, there will be laws preventing a father from preferring any of his children by will, and prescribing an equal division of his property at death. Laws on this subject will necessarily be dictated by the national genius and ideals and by social and economic conditions.

Where states have assumed the right to prescribe the rules of descent it has been usually based on the theory that the individual has an inherent right to accumulate and own property, but no vested or natural right to do as he pleases with it after it passes into other hands. In other words inheritance is a legal, not a natural, right, and may be regulated to suit the needs and purposes of the community.

Another important phase of this subject is the right of

the surviving wife. Originally among the Jews she could not own property or inherit from her husband. And yet while she had but few strictly legal rights her position in many cases was an important one in the family and tribe. The growth of laws relating to the rights of widows has been slow and gradual among all peoples, and makes a fascinating study which throws much light on their general progress in humanity and civilization.

1

Wills

There was little power of the disposition of property by will among the Jews. The law of Primogeniture prevailed, the oldest son taking the land and a double portion of the personalty. Wills, such as we know them in modern times were unknown. Perhaps it would be more accurate to say the power of disposition of property by will was in a very rudimentary state.

(D) Dt. 21 [16. 17.]

"Then it shall be, in the day that he causeth his sons to inherit that which he hath, that he may not make the son of the beloved the firstborn before the son of the hated, who is the firstborn: but he shall acknowledge the firstborn, the son of the hated, by giving him a double portion of all that he hath: for he is the beginning of his strength; the right of the firstborn is his."

A father could convey property to his oldest son but could not deprive him of his legal share of the property or divert his share.

(D) Dt. 21 [15-17]

Yet Abraham gave all his property to Isaac who was not his oldest son.

(J) Gen. 25 [5]

"And Abraham gave all that he had unto Isaac."

To his other children he gave gifts.

(J) Gen. 25^{6}

"But unto the sons of the concubines, that Abraham had, Abraham gave gifts; and he sent them away from Isaac his son, while he yet lived, eastward, unto the east country."

A father could, however, divide his personal property among his children. In some cases he could transfer the birthright to another son.

(E) Gen. 21^{10}

"Wherefore she said unto Abraham, Cast out this handmaid and her son: for the son of this handmaid shall not be heir with my son, even with Isaac."

(J) Gen. 27^{37}

"And Isaac answered and said unto Esau, Behold, I have made him thy lord, and all his brethren have I given to him for servants; and with grain and new wine have I sustained him: and what then shall I do for thee, my son?"

1 Ch. 5^{1}
1 K. 11^{11ff}

But this was prohibited in the Deuteronomic Code.

(D) Dt. 21^{15-17}

2

Intestate Estates, Descent of Property to Heirs

The wife was not an heir of her husband, much less of a child dying before she did.

In some cases she seemed to descend as property to the next heir or owner of the land, a fact also related to the Levirate law.

Ruth 4^{1-12}

"Now Boaz went up to the gate, and sat him down there: and, behold, the near kinsman of whom Boaz spake came by; unto whom he said, Ho, such a one!

turn aside, sit down here. And he turned aside, and sat down.

And he took ten men of the elders of the city, and said, Sit ye down here. And they sat down.

And he said unto the near kinsman, Naomi, that is come again out of the country of Moab, selleth the parcel of land, which was our brother Elimelech's:

And I thought to disclose it unto thee, saying, Buy it before them that sit here, and before the elders of my people. If thou wilt redeem it, redeem it: but if thou wilt not redeem it, then tell me, that I may know: for there is none to redeem it besides thee; and I am after thee. And he said, I will redeem it.

Then said Boaz, What day thou buyest the field of the hand of Naomi, thou must buy it also of Ruth the Moabitess, the wife of the dead, to raise up the name of the dead upon his inheritance.

And the near kinsman said, I cannot redeem it for myself, lest I mar mine own inheritance: redeem thou my right of redemption on thee: for I cannot redeem it.

Now this was the custom in former time in Israel concerning redeeming and concerning exchanging, to confirm all things; a man plucked off his shoe, and gave it to his neighbor; and this was the manner of attestation in Israel.

So the near kinsman said unto Boaz, Buy it for thyself, and he drew off his shoe.

And Boaz said unto the elders, and unto all the people, Ye are witnesses this day, that I have bought all that was Elimelech's and all that was Chilion's and Mahlon's, of the hand of Naomi.

Moreover Ruth the Moabitess, the wife of Mahlon, have I purchased to be my wife, to raise up the name of the dead upon his inheritance, that the name of the dead be not cut off from among his brethren, and from the gate of his place: ye are witnesses this day.

And all the people that were in the gate, and the elders,

said, We are witnesses. Jehovah make the woman that is come into thy house like Rachel and like Leah, which two did build the house of Israel: and do thou worthily in Ephratah, and be famous in Bethlehem; and let thy house be like the house of Perez, whom Tamar bare unto Judah, of the seed which Jehovah shall give thee of this young woman."

The law of Primogeniture has been stated above.

(D) Dt. 21 [15-17]

Under the Levirate law the first son of the brother became heir of the first husband.

(D) Dt. 25 [5. 6.]

"If brethren dwell together, and one of them die, and have no son, the wife of the dead shall not be married without unto a stranger: her husband's brother shall go in unto her, and take her to him to wife, and perform the duty of a husband's brother unto her.

And it shall be, that the firstborn that she beareth shall succeed in the name of his brother that is dead, that his name be not blotted out of Israel."

Ruth 4 [10]

When there was no son the inheritance went to the daughters.

(P) Nu. 27 [6-8]

If there were neither son nor daughters the inheritance was much the same as under modern rules of collateral inheritance.

(P) Nu. 27 [5-11]

"And Moses brought their cause before the Lord.

And Jehovah spake unto Moses, saying,

The daughters of Zelophehad speak right: thou shalt surely give them a possession of an inheritance among their father's brethren; and thou shalt cause the inheritance of their father to pass unto them.

And thou shalt speak unto the children of Israel, saying, If a man die, and have no son, then ye shall cause his inheritance to pass unto his daughter.

And if he have no daughter, then ye shall give his inheritance unto his brethren.

And if he have no brethren, then ye shall give his inheritance unto his father's brethren.

And if his father have no brethren, then ye shall give his inheritance unto his kinsman that is next to him of his family, and he shall possess it: and it shall be unto the children of Israel a statute and ordinance, as Jehovah commanded Moses."

It will be observed no reference is made to the Mother's relatives.

In most modern states where there are no direct heirs the property passes to the brothers and sisters if living, if not to their children and so on down the collateral lines of descent.

The son of a concubine could inherit.

(E) Gen. 21[10]

Wherefore she said unto Abraham, Cast out this handmaid and her son: for the son of this handmaid shall not be heir with my son, even with Isaac."

1 Ch. 5[1]

On the other hand see

Ju. 11[2]

"And Gilead's wife bare him sons; and when his wife's sons grew up, they drove out Jephthah, and said unto him, Thou shalt not inherit in our father's house; for thou art the son of another woman."

A maid could be the heir of her mistress.

Pr. 30[23b]

"And a handmaid that is heir to her mistress."

And a slave could inherit.

(E) Gen. 15[1-4]

"After these things the word of Jehovah came unto Abram in a vision, saying, Fear not, Abram: I am thy shield and thy exceeding great reward.

And Abram said, O Lord Jehovah, what wilt thou give

me, seeing I go childless, and he that shall be possessor of my house is this Eliezer of Damascus?

And Abram said, Behold, to me thou hast given no seed: and, lo, one born in my house is mine heir.

And, behold, the word of Jehovah came unto him, saying, This man shall not be thine heir; but he that shall come forth out of thine own bowels shall be thine heir."

Also bondmen could be inherited.

(H) Lev. 25 [46]

The inheritance of one tribe could not be transferred to another tribe but each tribe keeps its own land.

(P) Nu. 36 [1-12]

"And the heads of the fathers' houses of the family of the children of Gilead, the son of Machir, the son of Manasseh, of the families of the sons of Joseph, came near, and spake before Moses, and before the princes, the heads of the fathers' houses of the children of Israel: and they said, Jehovah commanded my lord to give the land for inheritance by lot to the children of Israel: and my lord was commanded by Jehovah to give the inheritance of Zelophehad our brother unto his daughters.

And if they be married to any of the sons of the other tribes of the children of Israel, then will their inheritance be taken away from the inheritance of our fathers, and will be added to the inheritance of the tribe whereunto they shall belong: so will it be taken away from the lot of our inheritance.

And when the jubilee of the children of Israel shall be, then will their inheritance be added unto the inheritance of the tribe whereunto they shall belong: so will their inheritance be taken away from the inheritance of the tribe of our fathers.

And Moses commanded the children of Israel according to the word of Jehovah, saying, The tribe of the sons of Joseph speaketh right.

This is the thing which Jehovah doth command concerning the daughters of Zelophehad, saying, Let them be married to whom they think best; only in to the family of the tribe of their father shall they be married.

So shall no inheritance of the children of Israel remove from tribe to tribe: for the children of Israel shall cleave every one to the inheritance of the tribe of his fathers.

And every daughter, that possesseth an inheritance in any tribe of the children of Israel, shall be wife unto one of the family of the tribe of her father, that the children of Israel may possess every man the inheritance of his fathers.

So shall no inheritance remove from one tribe to another tribe; for the tribes of the children of Israel shall cleave every one to his own inheritance.

Even as Jehovah commanded Moses, so did the daughters of Zelophehad: for Mahlah, Tirzah, and Hoglah, and Milcah, and Noah, the daughters of Zelophehad, were married unto their father's brother's sons:

They were married into the families of the sons of Manasseh the son of Joseph; and their inheritance remained in the tribe of the family of their father."

A prince could give property to his sons which would then be their inheritance, but not to a servant.

Ezek. 46 16-17

"Thus saith the Lord Jehovah; If the prince give a gift unto any of his sons, it is his inheritance, it shall belong to his sons; it is their possession by inheritance.

But if he give of his inheritance a gift to one of his servants, it shall be his to the year of liberty; then it shall return to the prince; but as for his inheritance, it shall be for his sons."

A prince could not confiscate the inheritance of his people.

Ezek. 46 18

"Moreover the prince shall not take of the people's inheritance, to thrust them out of their possession; he shall give inheritance to his sons out of his own possession, that my people be not scattered every man from his possession."

Laws of inheritance refer chiefly to landed property. There was but little personal property of value. The land was the principal possession of the Hebrews.

3

Real Property

1. Definition and Historical Note.

By real property we mean land and the buildings and improvements attached to the land. This together with their flocks and herds constituted the principal possessions of the ancient Hebrews. They had not accumulated stores of wealth such as stocks of merchandise, money, expensive household furniture or luxuries. They had no factories and no banks. The nation was comparatively poor. On account of the uncertainty of rain and the barrenness of the soil they were in constant danger of famine. Many of the illustrations in their great prophetic literature were of the parched desert, and the joyfulness of the "earlier and the later rain," things that were of the utmost importance in their economic lives.

The Jews were given Canaan as an inheritance by Yahweh. To them it was a sacred land. They were taught to cherish it as part of their divine inheritance, and were forbidden to alienate it. They could not sell land to strangers, that is, foreigners. Even transfers from one tribe of the Jews to another were carefully prevented.

Originally Canaan was given to the various tribes by lot. The tribes retained permanently the lands thus acquired and in turn allotted them to individual owners. These individuals held title, however, only as representative of the tribe, not by absolute ownership and control.

To prevent foreign ownership the land could not be sold in perpetuity. Every sale had to provide for the redemption of the land in the year of jubilee or at the end of one year in cases of lands and houses in walled towns. Sales therefore were little more than mortgages running to the period of redemption. Transfers of land were not necessary as there was little accumulation of property and practically no moving about from one place to another. The Jews were pretty well anchored to their ancestral homes.

A thorough knowledge of Jewish life and national conditions will enable us to understand the following rules which were laid down for the use, control anl transfer of land.

2. Allotment Among Tribes.

Canaan by command of Jehovah was allotted among the various tribes.

(P) Nu. 26 [52-56]

"And Jehovah spake unto Moses, saying.

Unto these the land shall be divided for an inheritance according to the number of names.

To the more thou shalt give the more inheritance, and to the fewer thou shalt give the less inheritance: to every one according to those that were numbered of him shall his inheritance be given.

Notwithstanding, the land shall be divided by lot: according to the names of the tribes of their fathers they shall inherit.

According to the lot shall their inheritance be divided between the more and the fewer."

(P) Nu. 33 [54]

"And ye shall inherit the land by lot according to your families; to the more ye shall give the more inheritance, and to the fewer ye shall give the less inheritance: wheresoever the lot falleth to any man, that shall be his; according to the tribes of your fathers shall ye inherit."

(P) Nu. 36 ^{z}
Josh. 18 $^{2-10}$

"And there remained among the children of Israel seven tribes, which had not yet divided their inheritance.

And Joshua said unto the children of Israel, How long are ye slack to go to possess the land, which Jehovah, the God of your fathers, hath given you?

Appoint for you three men of each tribe; and I will send them, and they shall arise, and walk through the land, and describe it according to their inheritance; and they shall come unto me.

And they shall divide it into seven portions: Judah shall abide in his border on the South, and the house of Joseph shall abide in their border on the North.

And ye shall describe the land into seven portions, and bring the description hither to me; and I will cast lots for you here before Jehovah our God.

For the Levites have no portion among you: for the priesthood of Jehovah is their inheritance: and Gad and Reuben, and the half-tribe of Manasseh, have received their inheritance beyond the Jordan eastward, which Moses the servant of Jehovah gave them.

And the men arose, and went; and Joshua charged them that went to describe the land, saying, Go and walk through the land, and describe it, and come again to me; and I will cast lots for you here before Jehovah in Shiloh.

And the men went and passed through the land, and described it by cities into seven portions in a book; and they came to Joshua into the camp at Shiloh.

And Joshua cast lots for them in Shiloh before Jehovah: and there Joshua divided the land unto the children of Israel according to their divisions."

Title could not be transferred to another tribe by marriage or by sale. If sold it returned in the Jubilee.

(P) Nu. 36 $^{4-7}$

"And when the jubilee of the children of Israel shall

be, then will their inheritance be added unto the inheritance of the tribe whereunto they shall belong: so will their inheritance be taken away from the inheritance of the tribe of our fathers.

And Moses commanded the children of Israel according to the word of Jehovah, saying, The tribe of the sons of Joseph speaketh right.

This is the thing which Jehovah doth command concerning the daughters of Zelophehad, saying, Let them be married to whom they think best; only to the family of the tribe of their father shall they be married.

So shall no inheritance of the children of Israel remove from tribe to tribe: for every one of the children of Israel shall cleave every one to the inheritance of the tribe of his fathers."

The land was allotted to families.

(P) Nu. 33 [54]
Jos. 13 [7-33]
18 [8-10]

For the allotment of land after the exile see

Ezek. 45 [1-8], 46 [16-18], 47.

Share of Levites consisted of the cities and suburbs.

(P) Nu. 35 [2-5]
Jos. 21 [3-42]

Levites as individuals had no inheritance.

(D) Dt. 18 [1.2.]

3. Sale of land. Law against Perpetuities.

(P) Gen. 23 [7-20]
Jer. 32 [42a. 43. 44]

Under the Levitical Law the land could not be sold in perpetuity—that is the seller must reserve in his deed the right to redeem it upon payment of a stipulated sum.

(H) Lev. 25 [23-28]

"And the land shall not be sold in perpetuity; for the land is mine; for ye are strangers and sojourners with me.

And in all the land of your possession ye shall grant a redemption for the land.

If thy brother be waxed poor, and sell some of his possession, then shall his kinsman that is next unto him come, and shall redeem that which his brother hath sold.

And if a man have no one to redeem it, and he be waxed rich and find sufficient to redeem it; then let him reckon the years of the sale thereof, and restore the overplus unto the man to whom he sold it; and he shall return unto his possession.

But if he be not able to get it back for himself, then that which he hath sold shall remain in the hand of him that hath bought it until the year of jubilee: and in the jubilee it shall go out, and he shall return unto his possession."

In the case of houses in a walled city only one year was allowed for redemption, after which if not redeemed the land was held by the purchaser in perpetuity. The theory seems to have been that houses represented an accumulation of personal property rather than real property.

(H) Lev. 25 [29-31]

"And if a man sell a dwellinghouse in a walled city, then he may redeem it within a whole year after it is sold; for a full year shall he have the right of redemption.

And if it be not redeemed within the space of a full year, then the house that is in the walled city shall be made sure in perpetuity to him that bought it, throughout his generations: it shall not go out in the jubilee.

But the houses of the villages which have no wall round about them shall be reckoned with the fields of the country: they may be redeemed, and they shall go out in the jubilee."

The land itself could not be sold, only its produce computed to the year of Jubilee. This was the effect of these provisions.

(H) Lev. 25 [15. 16. 34.]

"According to the number of years after the jubilee thou shalt buy of thy neighbor, and according unto the number of years of the crops he shall sell unto thee.

According to the multitude of years thou shalt increase the price thereof, and according to the fewness of years thou shalt diminish the price of it: for the number of the crops doth he sell unto thee.

But the field of the suburbs of their cities may not be sold; for it is their perpetual possession."

(P) Lev. 27 [16-20]

"And if a man shall sanctify unto Jehovah part of the field of his possession, then thy estimation shall be according to the sowing thereof: the sowing of a homer of barley shall be valued at fifty shekels of silver.

If he sanctify his field from the year of jubilee, according to thy estimation it shall stand.

But if he sanctify his field after the jubilee, then the priest shall reckon unto him the money according to the years that remain, unto the year of the jubilee; and an abatement shall be made from thy estimation.

And if he that sanctified the field will indeed redeem it, then he shall add the fifth part of the money of thy estimation unto it, and it shall be assured to him.

And if he will not redeem the field, or if he have sold the field to another man, it shall not be redeemed any more."

In one case the title seems to have been inalienable—at least not subject to forced sale to the prince—what we designate to-day by the legal phrase, Eminent Domain. By this is meant the right of the state to seize lands for public purposes by paying proper compensation. If there was a forced sale the nearest kinsman had the right to buy.

Jer. 32 [7-15]

1 K. 21 [3-4]

"And Naboth said to Ahab, Jehovah forbid it me, that I should give the inheritance of my fathers unto thee.

And Ahab came into his house heavy and displeased because of the word which Naboth the Jezreelite had spoken to him: for he had said, I will not give thee the inheritance of my fathers. And he laid him down upon his bed, and turned away his face, and would eat no bread."

A Prince's gift to his servants shall be redeemed.

Ezek. 46[17]

"But if he give of his inheritance a gift to one of his servants, then it shall be his to the year of liberty; then it shall return to the prince: but as for his inheritance, it shall be for his sons.

The following were the rules established for the

4. Redemption of Lands. (See note at the head of this chapter.)

(H) Lev. 25[15. 16.]
25[8. 9. 10.]

"And thou shalt number seven sabbaths of years unto thee, seven times seven years; and there shall be unto thee the days of seven sabbaths of years, even forty and nine years.

Then shalt thou send abroad the loud trumpet on the tenth day of the seventh month; in the day of atonement shall ye send abroad the trumpet throughout all your land.

And ye shall hallow the fiftieth year, and proclaim liberty throughout the land unto all the inhabitants thereof: it shall be a jubilee unto you; and ye shall return every man unto his possession, and ye shall return every man unto his family."

(H) Lev. 25[24-34]
Jer. 32[6-15]
Ruth 4[1-4 7.]

The Levites might redeem land at any time.

(H) Lev. 25[32-33]

"Notwithstanding the cities of the Levites, the houses

of the cities of their possession, may the Levites redeem at any time."

Land sanctified to Jehovah, could be redeemed upon payment of the sum received plus 20%.

(P) Lev. 27 [14. 15]

"And when a man shall sanctify his house to be holy unto Jehovah, then the priest shall estimate it, whether it be good or bad: as the priest shall estimate it, so shall it stand.

And if he that sanctified it will redeem his house, then he shall add the fifth part of the money of thy estimation unto it, and it shall be his."

Land devoted to Jehovah—that is for the use of the priests—could not be redeemed.

(P) Lev. 27 [28]

"Notwithstanding, no devoted thing, that a man shall devote unto Jehovah of all that he hath, whether of man or beast, or of the field of his possession, shall be sold or redeemed: every devoted thing is more holy unto Jehovah."

If no redemption be made or if the field is sold to another no further redemption could be made.

(P) Lev. 27 [20-21]

"And if he will not redeem the field, or if he have sold the field to another man, it shall not be redeemed any more: but the field, when it goeth out in the jubilee, shall be holy unto Jehovah, as a field devoted; the possession thereof shall be the priest's."

Amount required to redeem.

(P) Lev. 27 [16-19]

5. Modes of Transfer and Recording.

A particular instance of a sale of real estate.

(P) Gen. 23 [7-20]

"And Abraham stood up, and bowed himself to the people of the land, even to the children of Heth.

And he communed with them, saying, If it be your

mind that I should bury my dead out of my sight, hear me, and entreat for me to Ephron the son of Zohar, that he may give me the cave of Machpelah, which he hath, which is in the end of his field; for the full price let him give it to me in the midst of you for a possession of a buryingplace.

Now Ephron was sitting in the midst of the children of Heth; and Ephron the Hittite answered Abraham in the audience of the children of Heth, even of all that went in at the gate of his city, saying,

Nay, my lord, hear me: the field give I thee, and the cave that is therein, I give it thee; in the presence of the children of my people give I it thee: bury thy dead.

And Abraham bowed down himself before the people of the land.

And he spake unto Ephron in the audience of the people of the land, saying, But if thou wilt, I pray thee, hear me: I will give the price of the field; take it of me, and I will bury my dead there.

And Ephron answered Abraham, saying unto him, My lord, hearken unto me: a piece of land worth four hundred shekels of silver; what is that betwixt me and thee? bury therefore thy dead.

And Abraham hearkened unto Ephron; and Abraham weighed to Ephron the silver, which he had named in the audience of the children of Heth, four hundred shekels of silver, current money with the merchant.

So the field of Ephron, which was in Machpelah, which was before Mamre, the field, and the cave which was therein, and all the trees that were in the field, that were in all the border thereof round about, were made sure: unto Abraham for a possession in the presence of the children of Heth, before all that went in at the gate of his city.

And after this, Abraham buried Sarah his wife in the cave of the field of Machpelah before Mamre, (the same is Hebron) in the land of Canaan.

And the field, and the cave that is therein, were made sure unto Abraham for a possession of a buryingplace by the children of Heth."

(1) *Deed and mode of transfer.*

Jer. 32 [9-14]

"And I bought the field that was in Anathoth of Hanamel my uncle's son, and weighed him the money, even seventeen shekels of silver.

And I subscribed the deed, and sealed it, and called witnesses, and weighed him the money in the balances.

So I took the deed of the purchase, both that which was sealed according to the law and custom, and that which was open; and I delivered the deed of the purchase unto Baruch, the son of Neriah, the son of Mahseiah, in the presence of Hanamel mine uncle's son, and in the presence of the witnesses that subscribed the deed of the purchase, before all the Jews that sat in the court of the guard.

And I charged Baruch before them, saying, Thus saith Jehovah of hosts, the God of Israel; Take these deeds, this deed of the purchase which is sealed, and this deed which is open, and put them in an earthen vessel; that they may continue many days."

Ruth 4 [3-11]

"And he said unto the near kinsman, Naomi, that is come again out of the country of Moab, selleth the parcel of land, which was our brother Elimelech's; and I thought to disclose it unto thee, saying, Buy it before them that sit here, and before the elders of my people. If thou wilt redeem it, redeem it: but if thou wilt not redeem it, then tell me, that I may know: for there is none to redeem it besides thee; and I am after thee. And he said I will redeem it.

Then said Boaz, What day thou buyest the field of the hand of Naomi, thou must buy it also of Ruth the Moabitess, the wife of the dead, to raise up the name of the dead upon his inheritance.

And the near kinsman said, I cannot redeem it for myself, lest I mar mine own inheritance; take thou my right of redemption on thee; for I cannot redeem it.

Now this was the custom in former time in Israel concerning redeeming and concerning exchanging, for to confirm all things; a man drew off his shoe, and gave it to his neighbor: and this was the manner of attestation in Israel.

So the near kinsman said unto Boaz, Buy it for thyself, and he drew off his shoe.

And Boaz said unto the elders, and unto all the people, Ye are witnesses this day, that I have bought all that was Elimelech's, and all that was Chilion's and Mählon's, of the hand of Naomi."

(2) *Delivery of Deed.*

Jer. 32 [12]

"And I delivered the deed of the purchase unto Baruch the son of Neriah, the son of Mahseiah, in the sight of Hanamel mine uncle's son, and in the presence of the witnesses that subscribed the book of the purchase, before all the Jews that sat in the court of the guard."

(3) *Recording Deed.*

Jer. 32 [14]

"Thus saith Jehovah of hosts, the God of Israel; Take these deeds, this deed of the purchase, which is sealed, and this deed which is open; and put them in an earthen vessel; that they may continue many days."

(4) *Mortgages.*

Neh. 5 [2-5]

"For there were that said, We, our sons, and our daughters, are many; let us get grain, that we may eat, and live.

Some also there were that said, We are mortgaging our fields, and our vineyards, and our houses: let us get grain, because of the dearth.

There were also that said, We have borrowed money

for the king's tribute, upon our fields and our vineyards.

Yet now our flesh is as the flesh of our brethren, our children as their children: and, lo, we bring into bondage our sons and our daughters to be servants, and some of our daughters are brought into bondage already: neither is it in our power to help it; for other men have our fields and our vineyards."

6. Sabbatical Year.

The custom of letting the land lie fallow is common throughout the East, made necessary no doubt by lack of fertilizers and knowledge of proper methods of rotating crops.

Enforced rest of land every seventh year.

(C) Ex. 23 [10. 11]

"And six years thou shalt sow thy land, and shalt gather in the increase thereof: but the seventh year thou shalt let it rest and lie fallow; that the poor of thy people may eat: and what they leave the beast of the field shall eat. In like manner thou shalt deal with thy vineyard and with thy oliveyard."

(H) Lev. 25 [1-7]

"And Jehovah spake unto Moses in mount Sinai, saying,

Speak unto the children of Israel, and say unto them, When ye come into the land which I give you, then shall the land keep a sabbath unto Jehovah.

Six years thou shalt sow thy field, and six years thou shalt prune thy vineyard, and gather in the fruits thereof: but in the seventh year shall be a sabbath of solemn rest for the land, a sabbath unto Jehovah: thou shalt neither sow thy field, nor prune thy vineyard.

That which groweth of itself of thy harvest thou shalt not reap, and the grapes of thy undressed vine thou shalt not gather; it shall be a year of solemn rest for the land.

And the sabbath of the land shall be for food for you;

for thee, and for thy servant and for thy maid, and for thy hired servant, and for thy stranger, who sojourn with thee.

And for thy cattle, and for the beasts that are in thy land, shall all the increase thereof be for food."

(H) Lev. 25 [20-22]

"And if ye shall say, What shall we eat the seventh year? behold, we shall not sow, nor gather in our increase: then I will command my blessing upon you in the sixth year, and it shall bring forth fruit for three years.

And ye shall sow the eighth year, and eat yet of the fruits, the old store; until the ninth year, until its fruits come in ye shall eat the old store."

7. Jubilee Year. (See note at the head of this chapter.)

Every fiftieth year was a Jubilee year, inaugurated by blowing the trumpet on the Day of Atonement. This was the tenth day of the seventh month—corresponding broadly to our month of October.

Land shall lie fallow.

(H) Lev. 25 [11. 12.]

"A jubilee shall that fiftieth year be unto you: ye shall not sow, neither reap that which groweth of itself in it, nor gather the grapes in it of the undressed vines.

For it is a jubilee; it shall be holy unto you: ye shall eat the increase thereof out of the field."

For redemption of land from sale during the year of Jubilee see ante.

4

Personal Property

By personal property is meant all property that is movable, as distinguished from real property which is fixed, such as houses and lands. As heretofore stated there were but little accumulations of personal property when the Torah was framed. We should expect accordingly but few laws relating to this subject.

1. *Sale of personal property.*

Sales recognized.

(H) Lev. 25 [14]

"And if thou sell aught unto thy neighbor, or buy of thy neighbor's hand, ye shall not wrong one another."

A father could divide personal property among his sons.

(D) Dt. 21 [16]

2. *Mortgages and Pledges of Personal Property.*

Children could be pledged as security for debt.

2 K. 4 [1-7]

"Now there cried a certain woman of the wives of the sons of the prophets unto Elisha, saying, Thy servant my husband is dead; and thou knowest that thy servant did fear Jehovah: and the creditor is come to take unto him my two children to be bondmen.

And Elisha said unto her, What shall I do for thee? tell me: what hast thou in the house? And she said, Thy handmaid hath not any thing in the house, save a pot of oil.

Then he said, Go, borrow thee vessels abroad of all thy neighbors, even empty vessels; borrow not a few.

And thou shalt go in, and shut the door upon thee and upon thy sons, and shalt pour out into all those vessels; and thou shalt set aside that which is full.

So she went from him, and shut the door upon her and upon her sons; they brought the vessels to her, and she poured out.

And it came to pass, when the vessels were full, that she said unto her son, Bring me yet a vessel. And he said unto her, There is not a vessel more. And the oil stayed.

Then she came and told the man of God. And he

said, Go, sell the oil, and pay thy debt, and live thou and thy sons of the rest."

Prohibition of pledge of Mill or upper Millstone.

(D) Dt. 24 [6]

"No man shall take the mill or the upper millstone to pledge: for he taketh a man's life to pledge."

If the debtor is poor the pledge must be returned before sundown.

(D) Dt. 24 [13]

"Thou shalt surely restore to him the pledge when the sun goeth down, that he may sleep in his garment and bless thee: and it shall be righteousness unto thee before Jehovah thy God."

(C) Ex. 22 [26. 27]

"If thou at all take thy neighbor's garment to pledge, thou shalt restore it unto him before the sun goeth down: for that is his only covering, it is his garment for his skin: wherein shall he sleep? and it shall come to pass, when he crieth unto me, that I will hear; for I am gracious."

Modern laws permit a pledge to be retained until the debt be paid. The contract pledging personal property as security for a debt may be a chattel mortgage, or an agreement of pledge, or hypothecation. Such contracts are common to-day.

A creditor must not go into the house of the debtor to procure a pledge.

(D) Dt. 24 [10. 11.]

"When thou dost lend thy neighbor any manner of loan, thou shalt not go into his house to fetch his pledge.

Thou shalt stand without, and the man to whom thou dost lend shall bring forth the pledge without unto thee."

Abuse of taking pledges:

Job 24 [3. 9]

"They drive away the ass of the fatherless; they take the widow's ox for a pledge.

There are that pluck the fatherless from the breast, and take a pledge of the poor."

3. *Redemption of pledges.*

(D) Dt. 24 [13]

5

Usury or Interest

The taking of interest for the loan of money was called usury in Bible times. At present usury is taking more than the legal rate of interest, the rate permitted being fixed by statute. As is well known the taking of interest was forbidden among Jews. The reason is apparent when we remember the economic conditions of the times. Money was not loaned for purposes of trade or investment but for the relief of the poor in cases of emergency. There was little personal property in existence, little personal credit, but little trade, great poverty. Loans under such conditions were a form of charity. They were not made for purposes of gain in business.

Compare the treatment of this subject of usury by Shakespeare in the Merchant of Venice.

(1) A Jew was forbidden to take usury from another Jew.

(C) Ex. 22 [25]

"If thou lend money to any of my people with thee that is poor, thou shalt not be to him as a creditor; neither shall ye lay upon him interest."

(D) Dt. 23 [19. 20.]

"Thou shalt not lend upon interest to thy brother; interest of money, interest of victuals, interest of any thing that is lent upon interest.

Unto a foreigner thou mayest lend upon interest; but unto thy brother thou shalt not lend upon interest, that

Jehovah thy God may bless thee in all that thou puttest thy hand unto in the land whither thou goest in to possess it."

(H) Lev. 25 [36. 37.]

Social conditions.

Neh. 5 [10]

"And I likewise, my brethren and my servants, do lend them money and grain. I pray you, let us leave off this usury."

(2) Usury was allowed to be charged to foreigners.

(D) Dt. 23 [20b.]

(3) Penalty for charging.

Neh. 5 [11]

"Restore, I pray you, to them even this day, their fields, their vineyards, their oliveyards, and their houses, also the hundredth part of the money, and of the grain, the new wine, and the oil, that ye exact of them."

This is a restoration of the security for the loan plus one per cent penalty.

(4) Rate of Interest.

It may be interesting to compare rates of interest in other countries. These of course varied greatly in the same country from time to time.

In Babylon 20% for money.
For grain 25 to 33%.
For short loans as high as 300%.
In Egypt 30%.
In Greece 12% was considered low.

6

Debtor and Creditor

(1) *The relation of debtor and creditor was well recognized.* Debts were contracted chiefly in case of need, rather than for investment or trade.

(2) *Release of Debts.*

(1) This was commanded for the Sabbatical year.

(D) Dt. 15 [1-6 12-18]

"At the end of every seven years thou shalt make a release.

And this is the manner of the release: Every creditor shall release that which he hath lent unto his neighbor; he shall not exact it of his neighbor and his brother; because Jehovah's release hath been proclaimed.

Of a foreigner thou mayest exact it: but whatsoever of thine is with thy brother thy hand shall release."

Neh. 10 [31]

"And if the peoples of the land bring wares or any grain on the sabbath day to sell, that we would not buy of them on the sabbath, or on a holy day: and that we would forego the seventh year, and the exaction of every debt."

In the year of Jubilee.

Freeing of Servants.

(H) Lev. 25 [39-42]

"And if thy brother be waxed poor with thee, and sell himself unto thee; thou shalt not make him to serve as a bondservant.

As a hired servant, and as a sojourner, he shall be with thee: he shall serve with thee unto the year of jubilee; then shall he go out from thee, and his children with him, and shall return unto his own family, and unto the possession of his fathers shall he return.

For they are my servants, which I brought forth out of the land of Egypt: they shall not be sold as bondmen."

No release was granted to a foreigner.

(D) Dt. 15 [3]

"Of a foreigner thou mayest exact it: but whatsoever of thine is with thy brother thy hand shall release:"

No release could be granted if fraud was practiced.

Talmud.

To prevent a release a legal fiction was invented. If the creditor should make a declaration at the time of making a loan reserving the right to collect independent of the Jubilee requirements, these did not apply and the debt was not released in the year of Jubilee.

Talmud.

(3) *Moratorium and Statute of Limitations.*

In the late world war most nations declared a moratorium. This postponed the collection of debts in certain cases till after the termination of the war. Some writers suppose the Jubilee requirements were only a moratorium or suspension of the right to collect, during the year. The command, however, is in unequivocal terms and requires full cancellation of the debt.

In reality it was an ancient form of what we to-day call a Statute of Limitations. This provides that after a certain time, varying in different cases, a debt shall be outlawed—that is, it cannot be legally enforced. The debt is not paid but enforced collection cannot be made.

The enforcement of the law was evidently difficult.

(D) Dt. 15 [9-11]

7

Miscellaneous Contracts

Written contracts were unknown. Agreements were made in the presence of witnesses and consisted of a simple act of oral understanding. In this respect they differed from those used in ancient Babylonia where contracts were recorded on clay tablets, sometimes placed within larger tablets, which were deposited in the temple or palace library for record or safe keeping. After the Exile the Jews began to trade and to develop some primitive trade forms and usages, including a rudimentary banking or money changing. Numerous branches of the law then developed and foreign legal terms were introduced. For a thorough exposition of the corresponding laws in Babylonia see chapter 6 of Jastrow's *Civilization of Babylonia and Assyria.*

Weights and Measures.

(D) Dt. 25 [13-16]

"Thou shalt not have in thy bag diverse weights, a great and a small:

Thou shalt not have in thy house diverse measures, a great and a small:

A perfect and just weight shalt thou have; a perfect and just measure shalt thou have: that thy days may be long in the land which Jehovah thy God giveth thee.

For all that do such things, even all that do unrighteously, are an abomination unto Jehovah thy God."

8

Damages for Breach of Contract

(See Courts and Legal Procedure)

B

CRIMINAL LAW

1. CRIMES AND THEIR PUNISHMENT

Introductory Note

As the Jews were a theocracy, crime was regarded as an offense against Jehovah rather than against the State. The Decalogue, The Law of Holiness, the Book of the Covenant, and the Deuteronomic Code thus regarded crime as a religious and moral rather than a public offense. What we regard as crimes against society or the public were looked upon as sins against Jehovah. It is only in the modern sense that we have classified crimes as crimes against individuals, against decency and morality as well as crimes of a purely religious nature. Of the latter we have but comparatively few in modern codes.

The conception of crime was also family or tribal rather than individual. In the earliest times guilt was not regarded as purely personal but was imputed to the family or tribe to which the offender belonged. Punishment was accordingly social rather than personal. When in a later development this latter view became prevalent there were established certain cities of refuge to which a criminal might flee and be safe from punishment.

Punishments were at first barbarous, the death penalty being inflicted for many crimes we would consider venial. There is a curious parallel to this in England where two centuries ago there were over a hundred crimes punishable by death. In the earliest times human sacrifices were common. A growing humaneness and leniency led to the substitution of fines and imprisonment for the old cruel law of Lex Talionis.

There was a gradual development too in modes of legal procedure. It is evident that in later times a well ordered system of court procedure came into existence. Regular trials were had, both sides were heard and well considered rules of evidence applied before conviction for crime could be had. Thus the rights of individuals gradually grew in importance and a more highly developed form of society came into existence. By referring the punishments set out in this chapter to the codes under which they were prescribed, and the dates of these codes as set out in the preliminary chapter of this book, a good idea may be formed as to the extent and rapidity of the growth of humanitarian ideas as illustrated in Jewish law.

2. CRIMES AGAINST THE PUBLIC

(1) *Bribery.*

Forbidden.

(C) Ex. 23[8]

"And thou shalt take no bribe; for a bribe blindeth them that have sight, and perverteth the words of the righteous."

(D) Dt. 16[19b.]

"Neither shall thou take a bribe: for a bribe doth blind the eyes of the wise, and pervert the words of the righteous."

(D) Dt. 27[25]

"Cursed be he that taketh a bribe to slay an innocent person:"

(2) *Perjury.*

Forbidden.

(D) Dt. 5[20]

"Neither shalt thou bear false witness against thy neighbor."

(C) Ex. 20[16] 23[1]
(H) Lev. 19[12]
(D) Dt. 19[16-20]

"If an unrighteous witness rise up against any man to testify against him of wrong-doing, then both the men, between whom the controversy is, shall stand before Jehovah, before the priests and the judges that shall be in those days; and the judges shall make diligent inquisition; and, behold, if the witness be a false witness, and have testified falsely against his brother; then shall ye do unto him, as he had thought to do unto his brother: so shalt thou put the evil away from the midst of you.

And those which remain shall hear, and fear, and shall henceforth commit no more any such evil in the midst of you."

(3) *Defiance of Law.*

(P) Nu. 15 [30-31]
(D) Dt. 17 [12-13]

"And the man that doeth presumptuously, in not hearkening unto the priest that standeth to minister there before Jehovah thy God, or unto the judge, even that man shall die: and thou shalt put away the evil from Israel.

And all the people shall hear, and fear, and do no more presumptuously."

Penalty.

(D) Dt. 17 [12-13]

(4) *Perverting and Obstructing Justice.*

(C) Ex. 23 [1. 2. 6. 7.]
(H) Lev. 19 [15. 35. 36.]
(D) Dt. 16 [19a.]

3. CRIMES AGAINST MORALITY

(1) *Adultery.*

(C) Ex. 20 [14]

"Thou shalt not commit adultery."

(D) Dt. 5 [18] 22 [22-24]
(H) Lev. 18 [20]
20 [10]

(P) Nu. 5 12b. 13a. 15. 18. 21-31

Penalty.

(D) Dt. 22 20-25

Death.

(H) Lev. 20 10

"And the man that committeth adultery with another man's wife, even he that committeth adultery with his neighbor's wife, the adulterer and the adulteress shall surely be put to death."

(2) *Rape.*

(D) Dt. 22 25-26

"But if the man find the damsel that is betrothed in the field, and the man force her, and lie with her; then the man only that lay with her shall die: but unto the damsel thou shalt do nothing; there is in the damsel no sin worthy of death: for as when a man riseth against his neighbor, and slayeth him, even so is this matter:"

(3) *Prostitution.*

(H) Lev. 19 20-22. 29.
21 9. 15

(D) Dt. 23 17a.

"There shall be no prostitute of the daughters of Israel."

(D) Dt. 23 18.

Penalty.

(H) Lev. 21 9

"And the daughter of any priest, if she profane herself by playing the harlot, she profaneth her father: she shall be burnt with fire."

(4) *Seduction.*

(C) Ex. 22 16. 17.
(D) Dt. 22 28. 29.

(5) *Incest.*

List of persons—

(H) Lev. 18 6-18.
(D) Dt. 22 30
27 20. 22. 23.

Penalty, death—

(H) Lev. 20 11. 12. 14. 17. 20. 21.

(6) *Woman Impure.*

(H) Lev. 18 [19]

20 [18]

(7) *Lying.*

(H) Lev. 19 [11b]

(8) *Covetousness.*

(C) Ex. 20 [17]

(D) Dt. 5 [21]

(9) *Wearing Dress of Other Sex.*

(D) Dt. 22 [5]

(10) *Indecent Assault.*

(D) Dt. 25 [11-12]

(11) *Sodomy.*

(D) Dt. 23 [17b.]

(H) Lev. 18 [22] 20 [13]

Penalty.

(C) Ex. 22 [19]

(12) *Bestiality.*

(C) Ex. 22 [19]

(D) Dt. 27 [21]

(H) Lev. 18 [23] 20 [15. 16.]

4. CRIMES AGAINST PERSONS

(1) *Murder.*

(C) Ex. 20 [13]

"Thou shalt not kill."

(P) Gen. 9 [5. 6.]

(C) Ex. 21 [12-15. 20. 21. 23.]

(D) Dt. 5 [17]

(D) Dt. 19 [11-13]

(H) Lev. 24 [17. 21b.]

(P) Nu. 35 [15. 33.]

Penalties.

Death for premeditated murder.

(C) Ex. 21 [12. 14.]

"He that smiteth a man, so that he dieth, shall surely be put to death."

"And if a man come presumptuously upon his neighbor, to slay him with guile; thou shalt take him from mine altar, that he may die."

Murder by instrument.

(P) Nu. 35 16-21

"But if he smote him with an instrument of iron, so that he died, he is a murderer: the murderer shall surely be put to death.

And if he smote him with a stone in the hand, whereby a man may die, and he died, he is a murderer: the murderer shall surely be put to death.

Or if he smote him with a weapon of wood in the hand, whereby a man may die, and he died, he is a murderer: the murderer shall surely be put to death.

The avenger of blood shall himself put the murderer to death: when he meeteth him, he shall put him to death.

But if he thrust him of hatred, or hurled at him, lying in wait, so that he died; or in enmity smote him with his hand, so that he died; he that smote him shall surely be put to death; he is a murderer; the avenger of blood shall put the murderer to death, when he meeteth him."

Killing father or mother.

(C) Ex. 21 15

"And he that smiteth his father, or his mother, shall be surely put to death."

Causing death by miscarriage.

(C) Ex. 21 22. 23

Sacrificing child to Molech.

(H) Lev. 20 2-5

"Moreover thou shalt say to the children of Israel, Whosoever he be of the children of Israel, or of the strangers that sojourn in Israel, that giveth of his seed unto Molech; he shall surely be put to death: the people of the land shall stone him with stones.

I also will set my face against that man, and will cut

him off from among his people; because he hath given of his seed unto Molech, to defile my sanctuary, and to profane my holy name.

And if the people of the land do at all hide their eyes from that man, when he giveth of his seed unto Molech, and put him not to death; then I will set my face against that man, and against his family, and will cut him off, and all that play the harlot after him, to play the harlot with Molech, from among their people."

(2) *Manslaughter.*

It will be observed that the Jewish Law recognized the different degrees of guilt where human life was taken, a distinction worked out carefully in all modern codes. Where the killing was without premeditation the offense was called manslaughter, as it is to-day.

(C) Ex. 21 [13]

"And if a man lie not in wait, but God deliver him into his hand; then I will appoint thee a place whither he shall flee."

(P) Nu. 35 [15]

"And Jehovah spake unto Moses, saying,

For the children of Israel, and for the stranger, and for the sojourner among them; shall these six cities be for refuge; that every one that killeth any person unwittingly may flee thither."

(D) Dt. 19 [4-6]

Penalty.

(C) Ex. 21 [18. 19. 20.]
(P) Nu. 35 [6]
Nu. 35 [9-15. 22-28]
(D) Dt. 19 [11-13]

(2a) *Self-defense.*

The right of self-defense seems to have been recognized.

(C) Ex. 22 [2]

(3) *Rape.*

(D) Dt. 22 [25-27]

(4) *Seduction.*

(C) Ex. 22 16. 17
(D) Dt. 22 28. 29
(H) Lev. 19 20-22

(5) *Assault.*

(C) Ex. 21 18. 26. 27

"And if men contend, and one smite the other with a stone, or with his fist, and he die not, but keep his bed: if he rise again, and walk abroad upon his staff, then shall he that smote him be quit;"

And if man smite the eye of his servant, or the eye of his maid, and destroy it: he shall let him go free for his eye's sake."

"And if he smite out his manservant's tooth, or his maidservant's tooth; he shall let him go free for his tooth's sake."

(H) Lev. 24 19
(D) Dt. 27 24

Assault by a beast.

(C) Ex. 21 28-32.

(6) *Slander.*

(C) Ex. 23 1a.

"Thou shalt not take up a false report."

(H) Lev. 19 16

"Thou shalt not go up and down as a talebearer among thy people; neither shalt thou stand against the blood of thy neighbor; I am Jehovah."

(D) Dt. 22 13-21

(7) *Kidnaping.*

(E) Ex. 21 16

(8) *Using False Weights and Measures.*

(H) Lev. 19 35-37
(D) Dt. 25 13-16

(9) *Selling into Slavery for Theft.*

(C) Ex. 22 3b

"If he have nothing, then he shall be sold for his theft."

(10) *Other Crimes Punishable by Death.*

(1) *Cursing Father and Mother.*

(C) Ex. 21^{17}
(H) Lev. 20^{9}

(2) *Rebellious Son.*

(D) Dt. 21^{18-21}

"If a man have a stubborn and rebellious son, that will not obey the voice of his father, or the voice of his mother, and, though they chasten him, will not hearken unto them: then shall his father and his mother lay hold on him, and bring him unto the elders of his city, and unto the gate of his place; and they shall say unto the elders of his city, This our son is stubborn and rebellious, he will not obey our voice; he is a glutton and a drunkard. And all the men of his city shall stone him to death with stones; so shalt thou put away the evil from the midst of thee; and all Israel shall hear, and fear."

(3) *Stealing and Selling a Man.*

(C) Ex. 21^{16}

"And he that stealeth a man, and selleth him, or if he be found in his hand, he shall surely be put to death."

(4) *Death Caused by Unruly Animal.*

(C) Ex. 21^{29}

"But if the ox were wont to gore in time past, and it hath been testified to his owner, and he hath not kept it in, but it hath killed a man or a woman; the ox shall be stoned, and its owner also shall be put to death."

(5) *Sorcery.*

(C) Ex. 22^{18}

"Thou shalt not suffer a sorceress to live."

(6) *Familiar Spirits.*

(H) Lev. 20^{27}

"A man also or a woman that hath a familiar spirit, or that is a wizard, shall surely be put to death: they shall stone them with stones; their blood shall be upon them."

(7) *False Prophet or Dreamer.*

(D) Dt. 13^{1-5}

"If there arise in the midst of thee a prophet, or a

dreamer of dreams, and he give thee a sign or a wonder, and the sign or the wonder come to pass, whereof he spake unto thee, saying, Let us go after other gods, which thou hast not known, and let us serve them; thou shalt not hearken unto the words of that prophet, or that dreamer of dreams: for Jehovah your God proveth you, to know whether ye love Jehovah your God with all your heart and with all your soul.

Ye shall walk after Jehovah your God, and fear him, and keep his commandments, and obey his voice, and ye shall serve him, and cleave unto him.

And that prophet, or that dreamer of dreams, shall be put to death, because he hath spoken rebellion against Jehovah your God, who brought you out of the land of Egypt, and redeemed thee out of the house of bondage, to draw thee out of the way which Jehovah thy God commanded thee to walk in. So shalt thou put away the evil from the midst of thee."

(D) Dt. 18 [20]

(8) *Apostasy.*

(D) Dt. 13 [6-16]
17 [5]

(9) *Sacrificing to other Gods.*

(C) Ex. 22 [20]

(10) *Refusing to Follow Decision of Judges.*

(D) Dt. 17 [12]

(11) *Blasphemy.*

(H) Lev. 24 [16]

"And he that blasphemeth the name of Jehovah, he shall surely be put to death; all the congregation shall certainly stone him: as well the sojourner, as the home-born, when he blasphemeth the name of Jehovah, shall be put to death."

(C) Ex. 20 [7]

(12) *Sabbath Desecration.*

(P) Nu. 15 [32-36]

"And while the children of Israel were in the wilderness, they found a man gathering sticks upon the sabbath day.

And they that found him gathering sticks brought him unto Moses and Aaron, and unto all the congregation.

And they put him in ward, because it had not been declared what should be done to him.

And Jehovah said unto Moses, The man shall surely be put to death: all the congregation shall stone him with stones without the camp.

And all the congregation brought him without the camp, and stoned him to death with stones; as Jehovah commanded Moses."

(13) *Unchastity.*

(D) Dt. 22 [21]

5. CRIMES AGAINST PROPERTY

(1) *Theft.*

(C) Ex. 20 [15]

"Thou shalt not steal."

(C) Ex. 22 [1. 7.]
(D) Dt. 5 [19]
(D) Dt. 23 [24. 25]

"When thou comest into thy neighbor's vineyard, then thou mayest eat of grapes thy fill at thine own pleasure; but thou shalt not put any in thy vessel.

When thou comest into thy neighbor's standing grain, then thou mayest pluck the ears with thy hand; but thou shalt not move a sickle unto thy neighbor's standing grain."

(P) Lev. 6 [2-7]
(H) 19 [11a.]

(2) *Burglary.*

(C) Ex. 22 [1-4]

"If a man shall steal an ox, or a sheep, and kill it, or sell it; he shall pay five oxen for an ox, and four sheep for a sheep.

If the thief be found breaking in, and be smitten so

that he dieth, there shall be no blood guiltiness for him.

If the sun be risen upon him, there shall be blood guiltiness for him; he shall make restitution: if he have nothing, then he shall be sold for his theft.

If the theft be found in his hand alive, whether it be ox, or ass, or sheep; he shall pay double."

Punishment by fine is prescribed by this passage.

(3) *Arson.*

(C) Ex. 22 [6]

"If fire break out, and catch in thorns, so that the shocks of grain, or the standing grain, or the field, are consumed; he that kindleth the fire shall surely make restitution."

(4) *Killing a Beast.*

(H) Lev. 24 [18. 21]

(5) *Removing Landmarks.*

(D) Dt. 19 [14]

"Thou shalt not remove thy neighbor's landmark, which they of old time have set, in thine inheritance which thou shalt inherit, in the land that Jehovah thy God giveth thee to possess it."

(D) Dt. 27 [17]
Prov. 23 [10]

(6) *Loss of Beast in Pit.*

(C) Ex. 21 [33. 34]

"And if a man shall open a pit, or if a man shall dig a pit, and not cover it, and an ox or an ass fall therein the owner of the pit shall make it good; he shall give money unto the owner thereof and the dead beast shall be his."

(7) *Trespass.*

(C) Ex. 22 [5]

"If a man shall cause a field or vineyard to be eaten, and shall let his beast loose, and it feed in another man's field; of the best of his own field, and of the best of his own vineyard, shall he make restitution."

(8) *Ox killing ox.*

(C) Ex. 21 [35-36]

6. CRIMES FOR WHICH NO PUNISHMENT WAS INFLICTED

(1) *Destroying the Eye of Servant.*

(C) Ex. 21 [26. 27.]

"And if a man smite the eye of his servant, or the eye of his maid, and destroy it; he shall let him go free for his eye's sake.

And if he smite out his manservant's tooth, or his maidservant's tooth; he shall let him go free for his tooth's sake."

(2) *Where an Ox Gores a Man to Death.*

(C) Ex. 21 [28]

(3) *For Killing a Burglar.*

(C) Ex. 22 [2]

(4) *If a Bailment Dies or Is Destroyed.*

(C) Ex. 22 [10. 11. 13.]

(5) *Loss of Hired Property.*

(C) Ex. 22 [15]

7. MODES OF PUNISHMENT

Different modes of punishment were employed, beginning with the lex talionis. A study of the following will illustrate the growth of more humane sentiments.

(1) *Lex Talionis.*

(P) Gen. 9 [6]

"Whoso sheddeth man's blood, by man shall his blood be shed: for in the image of God made he man."

(C) Ex. 21 [24. 25]

"Eye for eye, tooth for tooth, hand for hand, foot for foot, burning for burning, wound for wound, stripe for stripe."

(D) Dt. 19 [21]

(H) Lev. 24 [19-20]

(P) Nu. 35 [33]

For a murder no ransom (fine) was allowed.

(P) Nu. 35 [31]

"Moreover ye shall take no ransom for the life of a murderer, that is guilty of death; but he shall surely be put to death."

But ransom allowed in some cases.

(C) Ex. 21 [30]

"If there be laid on him a ransom, then he shall give for the redemption of his life whatsoever is laid upon him."

(2) *By Burning.*

(H) Lev. 20 [14]
21 [9]
(J) Gen. 38 [24]

"And the daughter of any priest, if she profane herself by playing the harlot, she profaneth her father; she shall be burnt with fire."

(3) *By Mutilation.*

(D) Dt. 25 [11. 12.]

(4) *By "Cutting off from People."*

(H) Lev. 17 [14] 18 [29]
20 [3. 4. 6. 17. 18.]
(P) Nu. 9 [13]
15 [30]
19 [13. 20.]

(5) *Hanging or Impaling.*

(D) Dt. 21 [22. 23.]

"And if a man have committed a sin worthy of death, and he be put to death, and thou hang him on a tree: his body shall not remain all night upon the tree, but thou shalt surely bury him that day; for he that is hanged is accursed of God; that thou defile not the land which Jehovah thy god giveth thee for an inheritance."

(6) *Stoning.*

(H) Lev. 24 [16] 20 [2. 27.]
(D) Dt. 17 [5]

"Then shalt thou bring forth that man or that woman,

who hath done this evil thing, unto thy gates, even that man or that woman; and thou shalt stone them to death with stones."

(D) Dt. 13 [10]
Dt. 21 [19. 20.]
22 [21.]
(P) Nu. 15 [32-36]

Witnesses to crime were to cast the first stone.

(D) Dt. 17 [7]

(7) *Scourging or Beating.*

(D) Dt. 25 [2-3]

"And it shall be, if the wicked man be worthy to be beaten, that the judge shall cause him to lie down, and to be beaten before his face, according to his wickedness, by number.

Forty stripes he may give him, he shall not exceed; lest, if he should exceed, and beat him above these with many stripes, then thy brother should seem vile unto thee."

(8) *Banishment.*

Ezra 7 [26]

(9) *Excommunication and Forfeiture.*

Ezra 10 [8]

"And that whosoever came not within three days, according to the counsel of the princes and the elders, all his substance should be forfeited, and himself separated from the assembly of the captivity."

In this case the property of the offender is forfeited to the treasury.

(10) *Imprisonment.*

Ezra 7 [26]
(H) Lev. 24 [12]
(P) Nu. 15 [34]

"And they put him in ward, that it might be declared unto them at the mouth of Jehovah."

2 Ch. 18 [25. 26.]
Jer. 20 [2]
29 [26]

(11) *Ordeal.*

(C) Ex. 22 [8]

(12) *Restitution.*

Return of property required plus 20%.

(H) Lev. 24 [18. 21]

(P) 5 [16]

6 [1-7]

(P) Nu. 5 [7]

For stolen or borrowed property.

(C) Ex. 22 [12. 14. 15.]

(13) *Compensation or Damages.*

(C) Ex. 21 [19. 32. 35. 36.]

"If he rise again, and walk abroad upon his staff, then shall he that smote him be quit: only he shall pay for the loss of his time, and shall cause him to be thoroughly healed."

"If the ox gore a manservant or a maidservant; there shall be given unto their master thirty shekels of silver, and the ox shall be stoned."

"And if one man's ox hurt another's, so that it dieth, then they shall sell the live ox, and divide the price of it; and the dead also they shall divide."

"Or if it be known that the ox was wont to gore in time past, and his owner hath not kept it in; he shall surely pay ox for ox; and the dead beast shall be his own."

(C) Ex. 22 [1. 3. 4. 5. 6.]

One should be punished for one's own sins—not for those of children or parents.

(D) Dt. 24 [16]

Person not to avenge his own wrongs.

(H) Lev. 19 [18]

Punishment was inflicted by the judges or in obedience to their orders.

(D) Dt. 25 [2]

8. AVENGER OF BLOOD

In a primitive state of society there is no official whose duty it is to execute punishments decreed by the proper authority. Among the Jews this duty in case of punishment by death was performed by what was known as the Avenger of Blood.

This was the nearest of kin in the family or tribe.

(D) Dt. 19 [12. 13.]

"Then the elders of his city shall send and fetch him thence, and deliver him into the hand of the avenger of blood, that he may die.

Thine eye shall not pity him, but thou shalt put away the innocent blood from Israel, that it may go well with thee."

(P) Nu. 35 [19.]

"The avenger of blood himself shall himself put the murderer to death; when he meeteth him, he shall put him to death."

2 Sam. 14 [7]

See also *Cities of Refuge.*

9. CITIES OF REFUGE

The mode of executing punishment by the blood avenger led to grave excesses and injustice. Sometimes an innocent man was slain. Gradually there grew up what were known as Cities of Refuge, whither a man charged with crime might flee and be safe from punishment. This protection and immunity was especially applicable in cases of accidental or unpremeditated killing.

The following passages show the operation of this scheme.

(1) Cities of Refuge appointed.

(D) Dt. 4 [41-43]

"Then Moses set apart three cities beyond the Jordan toward the sunrising; that the man slayer might flee thither, that slayeth his neighbor unawares, and hated him not in times past; and that fleeing unto one of these cities he might live: namely, Bezer in the wilderness, in the plain country, for the Reubenites; and Ramoth in Gilead, for the Gadites; and Golan in Bashan, for the Manassites."

Cities of Refuge first appear in this passage from Deuteronomy showing their origin far later than Moses, and originating no doubt in the advancing humane sentiment of a later age.

(D) Dt. 19^{1-13}
(P) Nu. $35^{6.\ 10-15}$
Jos. 20^{1-9}

When applicable.

(C) Ex. $21^{13.\ 14}$
(P) Nu. $35^{6.\ 9.\ 15.}$

No ransom was allowed for murder for man who fled to.

(P) Nu. $35^{31-32.}$

(2) The right to refuge was determined in the first instance by the priests of the temple or the elders of the city. Afterwards upon trial by the "Congregation."

(P) Nu. $35^{12.\ 24}$

"And the cities shall be unto you for refuge from the avenger, that the manslayer die not, until he stand before the congregation for judgment."

"Then the congregation shall judge between the smiter and the avenger of blood according to these ordinances."

Jos. $20^{4.\ 6.}$

"And he shall flee unto one of those cities and shall stand at the entrance of the gate of the city, and shall declare his cause in the ears of the elders of that city; and they shall take him into the city unto them, and give him a place, that he may dwell among them."

"And he shall dwell in that city, until he stand before the congregation for judgment, until the death of the high priest that shall be in those days: then shall the manslayer return, and come unto his own city, and unto his own house, unto the city from whence he fled."

If allowed he could remain till the death of the high priest and could then return home.

(P) Nu. 35 [25]

If he returned sooner he could be killed by the avenger.

(P) Nu. 35 [26-28]

RELIGIOUS LAW

I

NATIONAL DUTIES AND PROHIBITIONS

Historical Note on the Decalogue

There are three versions of the Ten Commandments or Decalogue, those found in Exodus 34, in Exodus 20, and in Deuteronomy 5. The earliest form is no doubt Exodus 34 which differs widely from the latter two, which are identical as to the ten commandments but differ as to their setting and the reasons upon which they are based. Originally they probably consisted of ten "Words," the simple form in which the Divine commands were set out. There is no satisfactory explanation for the version in Exodus 34. As primitive religions are proverbially ritualistic the Decalogue, at least in its expanded form in Exodus 20 and Deuteronomy 5, must have been a comparatively late development.

The Decalogue consists mostly of prohibitions. There are only two affirmative commands, to observe the Sabbath, and to honor father and mother. The high standard of morals and conduct set up by this noble Code has commanded universal admiration in all subsequent ages.

Here is the oldest form of the "Ten Words."

(J) Ex. 34 [12-26]

"Take heed to thyself, lest thou make a covenant with the inhabitants of the land whither thou goest, lest it be for a snare in the midst of thee:

But ye shall break down their altars, and dash in pieces their pillars, and ye shall cut down their Asherim (for thou shalt worship no other god: for Jehovah, whose name is Jealous, is a jealous God);

Lest thou make a covenant with the inhabitants of the land, and they play the harlot after their gods, and sacrifice unto their gods, and one call thee and thou eat of his sacrifice;

And thou take of their daughters unto thy sons, and their daughters play the harlot after their gods, and make thy sons play the harlot after their gods.

Thou shalt make thee no molten gods.

The feast of unleavened bread shalt thou keep. Seven days thou shalt eat unleavened bread, as I commanded thee, at the time appointed in the month Abib; for in the month Abib thou camest out from Egypt.

All that openeth the womb is mine; and all thy cattle that is male, the firstlings of cow and sheep.

And the firstling of an ass thou shalt redeem with a lamb: and if thou wilt not redeem it, then thou shalt break its neck. All the first-born of thy sons thou shalt redeem. And none shall appear before me empty.

Six days thou shalt work, but on the seventh day thou shalt rest; in plowing time and in harvest thou shalt rest.

And thou shalt observe the feast of weeks, even of the first-fruits of wheat harvest, and the feast of ingathering at the year's end.

Three times in the year shall all thy males appear before the Lord Jehovah, the God of Israel.

For I will cast out nations before thee, and enlarge thy borders; neither shall any man desire thy land, when thou goest up to appear before Jehovah thy God three times in the year.

Thou shalt not offer the blood of my sacrifice with leavened bread; neither shall the sacrifice of the feast of the passover be left unto the morning.

The first of the first-fruits of thy ground thou shalt bring unto the house of Jehovah thy God. Thou shalt not boil a kid in its mother's milk."

(1) *The Decalogue sets out the general law for the nation.*

(C) Ex. 20
(D) Dt. 5

(2) *The Jews to be a holy nation.*

(C) Ex. 19[6]

"And ye shall be unto me a kingdom of priests, and a holy nation. These are the words which thou shalt speak unto the children of Israel."

(C) Ex. 22[31] 23[24]
(H) Lev. 19[2]

"Speak unto all the congregation of the children of Israel, and say unto them, Ye shall be holy: for I Jehovah your God am holy."

(D) Dt. 7[6]

"For thou art a holy people unto Jehovah thy God: Jehovah thy God hath chosen thee to be a people for his own possession, above all peoples that are upon the face of the earth."

(D) Dt. 14[2. 21b]
26[18. 19.]

(3) *No heathen alliances permitted.*

(C) Ex. 23[31-33]

"And I will set thy border from the Red sea even unto the sea of the Philistines, and from the wilderness unto the River; for I will deliver the inhabitants of the land into your hand: and thou shalt drive them out before thee.

Thou shalt make no covenant with them, nor with their gods.

Thou shalt not dwell in thy land, lest they make thee sin against me: for if thou serve their gods, it will surely be a snare unto thee."

(D) Dt. 7[1-4]
(P) Ex. 34[12. 13. 15. 16.]

(4) *The Golden Rule.*

(H) Lev. 19[17. 18.]

"Thou shalt not hate thy brother in thy heart: thou shalt surely rebuke thy neighbor, and not bear sin because of him.

Thou shalt not take vengeance, nor bear any grudge against the children of thy people; but thou shalt love thy neighbor as thyself; I am Jehovah."

Compare the Golden Rule in the New Testament.

Mt. 7^{12}
$22^{35\text{-}40}$
Lk. 6^{31}

(5) *Apostasy and Idolatry.*

Apostasy was regarded as treason to the state as well as to Jehovah. We find here the foundations of the great doctrine of Monotheism.

(C) Ex. $20^{1\text{-}5}$

"And God spake all these words, saying,

I am Jehovah thy God, who brought thee out of the land of Egypt, out of the house of bondage.

Thou shalt have no other gods before me.

Thou shalt not make unto thee a graven image, nor any likeness of any thing that is in heaven above, or that is in the earth beneath, or that is in the water under the earth: Thou shalt not bow down thyself to them, nor serve them: for I Jehovah thy God am a jealous God, visiting the iniquity of the fathers upon the children, upon the third and upon the fourth generation of them that hate me:"

(C) Ex. $20^{22\text{-}26}$
20^{23}

"Ye shall not make other gods with me; gods of silver or gods of gold, ye shall not make unto you."

(C) Ex. $23^{13b.}$
(D) Dt. $5^{7\text{-}10}$
$6^{14.\ 15.}$
$13^{1\text{-}16}$
$4^{15\text{-}28}$ $8^{19.\ 20}$
$11^{16.\ 17.\ 26\text{-}28.}$

16 [21. 22.] 17 [2-7]
27 [15.] 30 [17. 18.]
(H) Lev. 26 [1] 19 [4]
(P) Ex. 34 [14. 17]

These were images of stone in the early days.

Jud. 17
1 Sam. 19 [13]

Erection of altars to Jehovah commanded.

(C) Ex. 20 [24-26]

These were ordered destroyed when they became centers of immorality.

(6) *Against Heathen Shrines and Rites.*

(C) Ex. 23 [24] 34 [12. 13.]
22 [20]
(D) Dt. 12 [2. 3. 29-31]
7 [5. 25.]
14 [1. 2.] 18 [9-12]
2 K. 23 [11] 10 [29]
2 Ch. 34 [4]
(H) Lev. 18 [3] 19 [27. 28]
20 [23]

(7) *Sabbath Laws.*

(C) Ex. 20 [8-11]

"Remember the sabbath day, to keep it holy.

Six days shalt thou labor, and do all thy work: but the seventh day is a sabbath unto Jehovah thy God: in it thou shalt not do any work, thou, nor thy son, nor thy daughter, thy manservant, nor thy maidservant, nor thy cattle, nor thy stranger that is within thy gates: for in six days Jehovah made heaven and earth, the sea, and all that in them is, and rested the seventh day: wherefore Jehovah blessed the sabbath day, and hallowed it."

(C) Ex. 23 [12] 31 [13b.-17]
34 [21] 35 [2. 3.]
(D) Dt. 5 [12-15]
(H) Lev. 19 [3b. 30.] 26 [2a.]
(P) Nu. 15 [32-36]

At first the law for Sabbath observance was social and humane rather than religious. Its religious character became intensified by the Babylonian Captivity. The penalty for Sabbath breaking was death.

(P) Nu. 15 [32-36]

(8) *Blasphemy.*

(C) Ex. 20 [7]

"Thou shalt not take the name of Jehovah thy God in vain: for Jehovah will not hold him guiltless that taketh his name in vain."

(C) Ex. 22 [28a.]
(D) Dt. 5 [11]
(H) Lev. 18 [21b.] 19 [12]
24 [10-13. 15b. 16. 23]

(9) *Desecration of Sacred Things.*

(P) Lev. 7 [20-21]

"But the soul that eateth of the flesh of the sacrifice of peace offerings, that pertain unto Jehovah, having his uncleanness upon him, that soul shall be cut off from his people.

And when any one shall touch any unclean thing, the uncleanness of man, or an unclean beast, or any unclean abomination, and eat of the flesh of the sacrifice of peace offerings, which pertain unto Jehovah, that soul shall be cut off from his people."

(H) Lev. 19 [30b.] 22 [3b.]
(P) Nu. 3 [38b.]
4 [17-20]
18 [22]

(10) *Sorcery and Witchcraft.*

(C) Ex. 22 [18]
(H) Lev. 19 [26b. 31.]
20 [6. 27.]

"And the soul that turneth unto them that have familiar spirits, and unto the wizards, to play the harlot after them, I will even set my face against that soul, and will cut him off from among his people."

"A man also or a woman that hath a familiar spirit, or that is a wizard, shall surely be put to death; they shall stone them with stones; their blood shall be upon them."

(11) *False Prophecy.*

(D) Dt. 18[18-22]

(12) *Sacrifice of Children Prohibited.*

This practice was common among the Canaanites and was usual in many instances by the Jews.

Jer. 7[31. 32]
19[5]
Ps. 106[37. 38]
(D) Dt. 12[29-31]
(H) Lev. 18[21a]

"And thou shalt not give any of thy seed to make them pass through the fire to Molech."

(H) Lev. 20[2-5]

"Moreover, thou shalt say to the children of Israel, Whosoever he be of the children of Israel, or of the strangers that sojourn in Israel, that giveth of his seed unto Molech; he shall surely be put to death: the people of the land shall stone him with stones.

I also will set my face against that man, and will cut him off from among his people; because he hath given seed of his seed unto Molech, to defile my sanctuary, and to profane my holy name.

And if the people of the land do at all hide their eyes from that man, when he giveth of his seed unto Molech, and put him not to death; then I will set my face against that man, and against his family, and will cut him off, and all that play the harlot after him, to play the harlot with Molech, from among their people."

(13) *Punishment by Jehovah if laws are not observed.*

(H) Lev. 26[14-39]

II

INDIVIDUAL CONDUCT

(1) *Love to God and Neighbor.*

(D) Dt. $6^{4.\ 5.}$ $10^{12.\ 19.}$
$11^{1.\ 13.}$
$30^{16.\ 19.\ 20.}$

(H) Lev. 19^{18}

"Thou shalt not take vengeance, nor bear any grudge against the children of thy people; but thou shalt love thy neighor as thyself: I am Jehovah."

This is the high water-mark of Old Testament Law.

(2) *Reverence and Gratitude.*

(D) Dt. 5^{29} 4^{10}
$6^{2.\ 24.\ 10\text{-}12}$
$8^{10.\ 19.\ 6.}$
$10^{12.\ 20.}$
13^{18} 14^{23}
17^{19} $31^{12.\ 13.}$

(3) *Covetousness.*

(C) Ex. 20^{17}
(D) Dt. 5^{21}

(4) *Lying Forbidden.*

(H) Lev. $19^{11b.}$

(5) *Cheating.*

(H) Lev. $19^{11b.}$

(6) *Duty to Honor Parents.*

(C) Ex. 20^{12}

"Honor thy father and thy mother, that thy days may be long in the land which Jehovah thy God giveth thee."

(D) Dt. 5^{16} 27^{16}
(H) Lev. $19^{3a.\ 32}$

(7) *To Give First Born Sons and First Fruits to Jehovah.*

(C) Ex. $22^{29\text{-}30}$

"Thou shalt not delay to offer of thy harvest, and of

the outflow of thy presses. The first born of thy sons shalt thou give unto me.

Likewise shalt thou do with thine oxen, and with thy sheep: seven days it shall be with its dam; on the eighth day thou shalt give it me."

(8) *To Act Justly.*

(c) Ex. 23[2. 3. 6.]

"Thou shalt not follow a multitude to do evil; neither shalt thou speak in a cause to turn aside after a multitude to wrest justice:

Neither shalt thou favor a poor man in his cause.

Thou shalt not wrest the justice due to thy poor in his cause."

(H) Lev. 19[15a. 35a.]

(9) *To Follow the Law.*

(D) Dt. 5[1. 31-33]
6[1-3. 6. 7. 17]
7[11] 8[1. 6. 11.]
10[12. 13.]
11[18. 19.]
26[16. 17.] 27[10. 26.]
30[15. 16.]

(H) Lev. 18[4. 5. 26.]
19[19] 20[8. 22.]
25[18]

(10) *Not to Mingle Animals, Seed or Garments.*

(D) Dt. 22[9-11]

(H) Lev. 19[19]

(11) *To Wear Reminders of the Law.*

(D) Dt. 6[8. 9.] 11[18-20] 22[12]

(P) Nu. 15[37-40]

HUMANE LAWS

In these regulations the Jews showed their superior moral ideals and standards to those of other ancient peoples. In fact these laws have few parallels in ancient times. The Jews first laid emphasis on persons rather than property. Such laws show the influence of the prophets.

1

Duties toward Persons

(1) *To Widows and Orphans.*
(C) Ex. 22$^{22-24}$
(D) Dt. 24^{17} 27^{19}

(2) *To Neighbors.*
(D) Dt. 22^{4}
(H) Lev. 19$^{13a. 18.}$

(3) *To the Poor.*
(C) Ex. 23$^{6.}$
(H) Lev. 19^{10}
(H) Lev. 25$^{35. 39. 43}$

(4) *To Sojourners.*
(C) Ex. 22^{21} 23^{9}
(H) Lev. 19$^{33. 34}$
(D) Dt. 10$^{18. 19}$
24$^{15. 17}$
27^{19}

(5) *To the Needy and Defenseless.*
(H) Lev. 19^{14}
(D) Dt. 24^{14}
(JE) 27^{18}

(6) *To Slaves and Servants.*
(D) Dt. 24$^{14. 15.}$
15$^{12-15}$
(C) Ex. 21^{2}
23^{12}

(7) *Reverence for the Aged.*
(H) Lev. 19^{32}

(8) *To Construct Battlement.*
(D) Dt. 22^{8}

(9) *Gleanings.*

Here we see the beginning of philanthropy, man's duty to be more than just.

(C) Ex. 23[10. 11.]
(H) Lev. 19[9. 10.]

"And when ye reap the harvest of your land, thou shalt not wholly reap the corners of thy field, neither shalt thou gather the gleaning of thy harvest.

And thou shalt not glean thy vineyard, neither shalt thou gather the fallen fruit of thy vineyard; thou shalt leave them for the poor and for the sojourner, I am Jehovah your God."

(H) Lev. 23[22]
(D) Dt. 24[19-21]

(10) *Sharing Offerings.*

(D) Dt. 16[10-14]
(H) Lev. 17[2-9]

2

Kindness to Animals

Here we find the first laws in history recognizing man's duty to the animal world. Individual kindness to animals of course always abounded, but was not commanded by law.

(1) *Beasts of Burden.*

(C) Ex. 23[12]

(2) *The Threshing Ox.*

(D) Dt. 25[4]

(3) *To Wild Animals.*

(C) Ex. 23[11]
(H) Lev. 25[5-7]

(4) *Mother and Young.*

(D) Dt. 22[6. 7.]
(H) Lev. 22[28]
(J) Ex. 34[26b.]

(5) *Return of Strays.*

(C) Ex. 23 4. 5.
(D) Dt. 22 1-4

CEREMONIAL LAW

Introductory Note

The Ceremonial Law of the Hebrews was contained for the most part in the Priestly Code, which as heretofore shown, and is included in the last chapters of Exodus, the whole of Leviticus, and part of Numbers, Genesis and Joshua. It was a most elaborate code, consisting of both important and minute regulations touching the entire religious and daily life of the individual and the nation.

This law was codified and arranged in its present form after the return from the Babylonian Exile, about the year 444 B. C., as has been virtually agreed upon by Biblical scholars. It was no doubt a codification of rules some of which had had a long prior origin, with the addition of many new ones. The concentration of the worship at Jerusalem magnified the importance of the priests and tended toward the development of an elaborate ritual.

As in all systems the ritual gradually acquired more importance in the eyes of those who practiced it than the realities of worship for which it stood and which it was designed to cultivate. It became encrusted in a rigid system to disregard which became a serious offense.

The Ceremonial Law represents the latest form of Judaism, the form used after the Jewish state had by the force of events been transformed into the Jewish church. In that form it existed in the time of Jesus, hence his fierce denunciations of the Scribes and Pharisees, who had regard to the form of these observances to the minutest detail, often to the neglect of the "weightier matters of the law."

Occasional reference will be made for purposes of

convenience and contrast to those rules existing before the Exile and those after.

A

JEWISH FEASTS

Festivals constituted the central feature of nearly all ancient religious life. In some countries the sun was worshiped. In others the moon was the central object of worship. The latter dates from the earliest times.

Job 31 [26]

The feasts of the Jews were held at the time of the full moon and it was the phases of the moon that gave rise to an observance of the seventh day. Later the prophets tried to give to these nature festivals a spiritual and ethical significance. After the Exile moon worship was abandoned, the Sabbath was fixed at every seventh day and it became a purely religious observance. Its relative importance was enhanced by the fact that in captivity the Jews were unable to observe many of their other feasts or their rules as to clean and unclean, while the Sabbath remained the one religious event that could be observed at all places and in all conditions of national or individual life. It was then ascribed to Moses which increased its solemnity and authority. Thus it became central in their system of worship.

1. *The Sabbath*

As prescribed in the Decalogue.

(E) Ex. 20 [8-11]

"Remember the sabbath day, to keep it holy.

Six days shalt thou labor, and do all thy work: but the seventh day is a sabbath of Jehovah thy God: in it thou shalt not do any work, thou, nor thy son, nor thy daughter, thy manservant, nor thy maidservant, nor thy cattle, nor thy stranger that is within thy gates: for in six days

Jehovah made heaven and earth, the sea, and all that in them is, and rested the seventh day: wherefore Jehovah blessed the sabbath day, and hallowed it."

(C) Ex. 23 [12]
34 [21]
35 [2]
(D) Dt. 5 [12-15]
Amos 8 [5]
Jer. 17 [21. 22.]

After the exile.

(H) Lev. 19 [3b. 30.]
23 [3] 26 [2]
(P) Nu. 15 [32-36]
28 [9. 10.]
(P) Gen. 2 [2. 3.]
(P) Ex. 16 [22-26] 35 [1-3]
(P) 31 [12-17]

2. *The Passover*

(JE) Ex. 12 [25-27a.]
(P) Ex. 12 [1-14 43-44. 48]
34 [25b.]
(D) Dt. 16 [1-8]

Males must offer worship three times a year—on the following three feasts.

(C) Ex. 23 [17]
(J) 34 [23]
(D) Dt. 16 [16]

Of Unleavened Bread.

This was the first of three great festivals and was celebrated at the time when the first sickle was put into the ripening grain.

(J) Ex. 13 [3-10]

"And Moses said unto the people, Remember this day, in which ye came out from Egypt, out of the house of bondage; for by strength of hand Jehovah brought you out from this place: there shall no leavened bread be eaten.

This day came ye forth in the month Abib.

And it shall be when Jehovah shall bring thee into the land of the Canaanite, and the Hittite, and the Amorite, and the Hivite, and the Jebusite, which he sware unto thy fathers to give thee, a land flowing with milk and honey, thou shalt keep this service in this month.

Seven days thou shalt eat unleavened bread, and in the seventh day shall be a feast to Jehovah.

Unleavened bread shall be eaten throughout the seven days; and there shall no leavened bread be seen with thee, neither shall there be leaven seen with thee, in all thy borders.

And thou shalt tell thy son in that day, saying, It is because of that which Jehovah did for me when I came forth out of Egypt.

And it shall be for a sign unto thee upon thy hand, and for a memorial between thine eyes, that the law of Jehovah may be in thy mouth: for with a strong hand hath Jehovah brought thee out of Egypt.

Thou shalt therefore keep this ordinance in its season from year to year."

(C) Ex. 23 [14. 15.]
(J) 34 [18]
(D) Dt. 16 [3. 4a. 8a.]
Jos. 5 [10]
2 Chr. 30 [5-9]
35 [6]

After the Exile.

(P) Ex. 12 [1-20]

"And Jehovah spake unto Moses and Aaron in the land of Egypt, saying,

This month shall be unto you the beginning of months: it shall be the first month of the year to you.

Speak ye unto all the congregation of Israel, saying, In the tenth day of this month they shall take to them every man a lamb, according to their fathers' houses, a lamb for a household:

And if the household be too little for a lamb, then shall he and his neighbor next unto his house take one according to the number of the souls: according to every man's eating ye shall make your count for the lamb.

Your lamb shall be without blemish, a male a year old: ye shall take it out from the sheep, or from the goats: and ye shall keep it until the fourteenth day of the same month: and the whole assembly of the congregation of Israel shall kill it at even.

And they shall take of the blood, and put it on the two side-posts and on the lintel, upon the houses wherein they shall eat it.

And they shall eat the flesh in that night, roast with fire, and unleavened bread; with bitter herbs they shall eat it.

Eat not of it raw, nor boiled at all with water, but roast with fire; its head with its legs, and with the inwards thereof.

And ye shall let nothing of it remain until the morning; but that which remaineth of it until the morning ye shall burn with fire.

And thus shall ye eat it; with your loins girded, your shoes on your feet, and your staff in your hand; and ye shall eat it in haste: it is Jehovah's passover.

For I will go through the land of Egypt in that night, and will smite all the firstborn in the land of Egypt, both man and beast; and against all the gods of Egypt I will execute judgments: I am Jehovah.

And the blood shall be to you for a token upon the houses where ye are: and when I see the blood, I will pass over you, and there shall be no plague upon you to destroy you, when I smite the land of Egypt.

And this day shall be unto you for a memorial, and ye shall keep it a feast to Jehovah; throughout your generations ye shall keep it a feast by an ordinance for ever.

Seven days shall ye eat unleavened bread; even the first day ye shall put away leaven out of your houses: for whosoever eateth leavened bread from the first day until the seventh day, that soul shall be cut off from Israel.

And in the first day there shall be to you a holy convocation, and in the seventh day a holy convocation; no manner of work shall be done in them, save that which every man must eat, that only may be done of you.

And ye shall observe the feast of unleavened bread; for in this selfsame day have I brought your hosts out of the land of Egypt: therefore shall ye observe this day in your generations by an ordinance for ever.

In the first month, on the fourteenth day of the month at even, ye shall eat unleavened bread, until the one and twentieth day of the month at even.

Seven days shall there be no leaven found in your houses: for whosoever eateth that which is leavened, even that soul shall be cut off from the congregation of Israel, whether he be a sojourner, or one that is born in the land.

Ye shall eat nothing leavened; in all your habitations shall ye eat unleavened bread."

(P) Ex. 12 [43. 45-50]

(H) Lev. 23 [4-8]

"These are the set feasts of Jehovah, even holy convocations, which ye shall proclaim in their season.

In the first month on the fourteenth day of the month at even, is Jehovah's passover.

And on the fifteenth day of the same month is the feast of unleavened bread unto Jehovah: seven days ye shall eat unleavened bread.

In the first day ye shall have a holy convocation: ye shall do no servile work.

But ye shall offer an offering made by fire unto Jehovah seven days: in the seventh day is a holy convocation: ye shall do no servile work."

(P) Nu. 9^{1-14}
(P) 28^{16-25}

Punishment for refusal to celebrate.

(P) Nu. 9^{13}

3. *Feast of Weeks—First Fruits*

This occurred seven weeks after the feast of Unleavened Bread.

(C) Ex. $23^{14.\ 16a.}$

"Three times thou shalt keep a feast unto me in the year."

"And the feast of harvest, the first fruits of thy labors, which thou sowest in the field:"

(D) Dt. 16^{9-12}
(H) Lev. 23^{15-21}
(J) Ex. 34^{22}

After the exile.

(P) Nu. 28^{26-28}

4. *The Feast of Ingathering or Tabernacles*

In the early codes the date of this feast was indeterminate. It came at the end of the harvest and was celebrated for a week in length at Jerusalem. It was their most important feast and corresponded with our Thanksgiving.

(C) Ex. 23^{16b}

"And the feast of ingathering, at the end of the year, when thou gatherest in thy labors out of the field."

(D) Dt. 16^{13-17}
(J) Ex. $34^{22b.}$
Ezra 3^{4}
1 K. 8^{2}
2 Chr. 5^{3}

Booths.

(H) Lev. 23^{42}

After the exile.
15th day, 7th month—Lev. 23 $^{33-36\ 39-44}$
(P) Nu. 29 $^{12-38}$

5. *Sabbatical Year*

(C) Ex. 23 $^{10-12}$

"And six years thou shalt sow thy land, and shalt gather in the increase thereof: but the seventh year thou shalt let it rest and lie fallow that the poor of thy people may eat: and what they leave the beast of the field shall eat. In like manner thou shalt deal with thy vineyard, and with thy oliveyard."

(D) Dt. 15 $^{1-2}$
Jer. 34 $^{12-16}$

After the exile.
(H) Lev. 25 $^{1-5\ 20-22}$

Post Exilic Feasts

The exile changed greatly the life of the Jews. Feasts became occasions of gloom instead of rejoicing. To gain Jehovah's favor—long lost, they adopted fasting and an elaborate ritual. Detached festivals of an agricultural nature became fixed as to their dates. New feasts were added, and there was a steady trend toward a strict observance of ceremonial rites.

6. *New Moon*

At first a family observance, the feast of the New Moon now becomes a ceremonial function.

(P) Nu. 28 $^{11-15}$
Ezek. 46 ^{3}

7. *Atonement*

The fast known as the Atonement is not found before the Exile or in the Holiness Code. It occurs in one of the latest sections of the Pentateuch. This great fast came from a sense of national guilt produced by the captivity and national misfortunes. Its observance was to remove all sin otherwise overlooked, and thus it became a great national confession for both national and individual sins. It became the most important of all religious rites among later Jews, and remains so still.

(P) Ex. 30 [10]
(P) Lev. 16 For priest 1-14
For people 15-22
Scapegoat.

Date of

(P) Lev. 16 [29. 30.]

"And it shall be a statute for ever unto you: in the seventh month, on the tenth day of the month, ye shall afflict your souls, and shall do no manner of work, the home-born, or the stranger that sojourneth among you: for on this day shall atonement be made for you, to cleanse you; from all your sins shall ye be clean before Jehovah."

(H) Lev. 23 [26-32]

"And Jehovah spake unto Moses, saying,

Howbeit on the tenth day of this seventh month is the day of atonement: it shall be a holy convocation unto you, and ye shall afflict your souls; ye shall offer an offering made by fire unto Jehovah.

And ye shall do no manner of work in that same day: for it is a day of atonement, to make atonement for you before Jehovah your God.

For whatsoever soul it be that shall not be afflicted in that same day: he shall be cut off from his people.

And whatsoever soul it be that doeth any manner of work in that same day, that soul will I destroy from among his people.

Ye shall do no manner of work; it is a statute for ever throughout your generations in all your dwellings.

It shall be unto you a sabbath of solemn rest, and ye shall afflict your souls; in the ninth day of the month at even, from even unto even, shall ye keep your sabbath."

(H) Lev. 25 [9]

(P) Nu. 29 [7-11]

8. *Trumpets*

This feast did not exist before the Exile. By ordinance it became the First Day of the New Year.

(H) Lev. 23 [23-25]

(P) Nu. 29 [1-6]

"And in the seventh month, on the first day of the month, ye shall have a holy convocation; ye shall do no servile work: it is a day of blowing of trumpets unto you.

And ye shall offer a burnt offerng for a sweet savor unto Jehovah: one young bullock, one ram, and seven he-lambs a year old without blemish: and their meal-offering, fine flour mingled with oil, three tenth parts for the bullock, two tenth parts for the ram, and one tenth part for every lamb of the seven lambs: and one he-goat for a sin offering, to make atonement for you: besides the burnt offering of the new moon, and the meal offering thereof and the continual burnt offering and the meal offering thereof, and their drink offerings, according unto their ordinance, for a sweet savor, an offering made by fire unto Jehovah."

(P) Nu. 10 [10]

9. *Year of Jubilee*

(H) Lev. 25 [8-16. 23-34. 39-42. 47-52. 54]

B

SACRIFICES

Introductory Note

Sacrifice has held a chief place in all natural religions. It was a primitive idea that God could be appeased and his favor secured by sacrificing to him the offerings of his helpless and sinful children. Thus sacrifice is as old as the human race. Man found himself in a world of wonder and mystery. The powers of nature filled him with awe. He did not understand nature's laws, but thought they were manifestations of an all-powerful and angry deity. In his ignorance and helplessness he sought to appease the divine wrath and secure the favor of his gods.

There were three main purposes in making sacrifices:

1. To secure favor.
2. To remove displeasure.
3. To express gratitude.

Man transferred to God his own passions and desires. Originally God was in the stone used as an altar and needed food. Hence the practice of giving food to the gods by means of sacrifice. There was another idea—that all meals were sacrifices made to the gods. The worshipers killed a valuable animal and brought their best cereals and fruits to some consecrated place. The rude altar was daubed with blood and the food was left for the god to eat. The savor of the burnt offering was pleasing to Jehovah. In ancient Greece killing a beast was always a sacrificial act. Roman families treated meals as sacrificial in character, leaving food at each meal for the family Lares.

Out of these ideas grew an elaborate system of ceremonial, a great ritual of sacrifice which finds its fullest expression in the Priestly Code. Every act was explicitly commanded and carefully described. The ritual of the priests became a complicated code, difficult to observe, and even to understand.

The place of sacrifice requires especial mention. Originally the summits of mountains or the tops of hills were used. These were called "High Places" and became very numerous. Nearly every hill had its sanctuary. Around these places of worship great abuses were developed. They became scenes of the grossest immoral practices. It was chiefly these abuses which called forth the stringent regulations of the Book of the Law in which all these High Places were ordered destroyed and all Hebrew worship centered in the temple at Jerusalem.

Another especial feature worthy of note is the fact that in early days human sacrifices were made. These were abolished by expresss command, and sacrifices confined to animals, cereals and fruit, and even in later times to the payment of a small sum of money, all of which developed a complete tithing system.

Read 1 Sam. 9.

I

KINDS OF SACRIFICIAL OFFERINGS

A. *Peace offerings.*

Ritual of: (P) Lev. 7 $^{11-18}$

"And this is the law of the sacrifice of peace offerings, which one shall offer unto Jehovah.

If he offer it for a thanksgiving, then he shall offer with the sacrifice of thanksgiving unleavened cakes mingled with oil, and unleavened wafers anointed with oil, and cakes mingled with oil, of fine flour soaked.

With the cakes of leavened bread, he shall offer his oblation with the sacrifice of his peace offerings for thanksgiving.

And of it he shall offer one out of each oblation for

a heave offering unto Jehovah; it shall be the priest's that sprinkleth the blood of the peace offerings.

And the flesh of the sacrifice of his peace offerings for thanksgiving shall be eaten the day of his oblation; he shall not leave any of it until the morning.

But if the sacrifice of his oblation be a vow, or a freewill offering, it shall be eaten on the day that he offereth his sacrifice; and on the morrow that which remaineth of it shall be eaten: but that which remaineth of the flesh of the sacrifice on the third day shall be burnt with fire.

And if any of the flesh of the sacrifice of his peace offerings be eaten on the third day, it shall not be accepted, neither shall it be imputed unto him that offereth it: it shall be an abomination, and the soul that eateth of it shall bear his iniquity."

(P) Lev. 7 [28-32]
3 [1. 6-17]
3 [1-5 herd]
3 [6-17 flock]
19 [5-8]
22 [21. 23]
17 [1-9]
(P) Ex. 29 [19-26]

B. *Sin Offering.*

(P) Lev. 5 [1-13]
4 [1-35]
8 [14. 15]
10 [16-20]

Ritual of— (P) Lev. 6 [24-30]

"And Jehovah spoke unto Moses, saying,

Speak unto Aaron and to his sons, saying, This is the law of the sin offering: in the place where the burnt offering is killed shall the sin offering be killed before Jehovah: it is most holy.

The priest that offereth it for sin shall eat it: in a holy place shall it be eaten, in the court of the tent of the meeting.

Whatsoever shall touch the flesh thereof shall be holy; and when there is sprinkled of the blood thereof upon any garment, thou shalt wash that whereon it was sprinkled in a holy place.

But the earthen vessel wherein it is boiled shall be broken: and if it be boiled in a brazen vessel, it shall be both scoured, and rinsed in water.

Every male among the priests shall eat thereof: it is most holy.

And no sin offering, whereof any of the blood is brought into the tent of the meeting to make atonement in the holy place, shall be eaten: it shall be burnt with fire."

Notice the Scape Goat offering for the sins of all Israel.

(P) Lev. 16 [20-22]

"And when he hath made an end of atoning for the holy place, and the tent of the meeting and the altar, he shall present the live goat; and Aaron shall lay both his hands upon the head of the live goat, and confess over him all the iniquities of the children of Israel, and all their transgressions, even all their sins; and he shall put them upon the head of the goat, and shall send him away by the hand of a man that is in readiness into the wilderness: and the goat shall bear upon him all their iniquities unto a solitary land: and he shall let go the goat in the wilderness."

(P) Nu. 15 [22-31]
(P) Ex. 29 [11-14]

Red Heifer.

Very ancient. This was probably a part of their sanitary regulations.

(P) Nu. 19 [2]

C. *Guilt or Trespass Offering.*

Very ancient.

(P) Lev. 5 [14-19]
6 [1-7]
7 [1-7]

"And this is the law of the trespass offering: it is most holy.

In the place where they kill the burnt offering shall they kill the trespass offering: and the blood thereof shall be sprinkled upon the altar round about.

And he shall offer of it all the fat thereof: the fat tail, and the fat that covereth the inwards, and the two kidneys, and the fat that is on them, which is by the loins, and the caul upon the liver, with the kidneys, shall he take away; and the priest shall burn them upon the altar for an offering made by fire unto Jehovah: it is a trespass offering.

Every male among the priests shall eat thereof: it shall be eaten in a holy place; it is most holy.

As is the sin offering, so is the trespass offering; there is one law for them: the priest that maketh atonement therewith, he shall have it."

(H) Lev. 19^{20-22}
(P) Nu. 5^{5-8}

For ignorance.

(P) Nu. 15^{24-28}

D. *Leprosy Offering.*

(P) Lev. 13^{59}
$14^{2-32\ 43-57}$

E. *Burnt Offering.*

Of Herd

(P) Lev. 1^{3-9}

Flock 1^{10-13}
Birds 1^{14-17}
Ritual of 6^{2-13}
See also

(J) Ex. 18^{12}
(P) 29^{15-18}
1 K. 3^{4}

Daily Offering.

(P) Ex. 29^{38-42}
$30^{7\ 8}$.

(P) Nu. 28 1-8

F. *Meal Offering.*

Of Flour (P) Lev. 2 1-3

Baked 2 4-10

First Fruits 2 14-16

Leaven forbidden 2 10-13

Ritual of

(P) Lev. 6 14-23

"And this is the law of the meal offering: The sons of Aaron shall offer it before Jehovah, before the altar.

And he shall take up therefrom his handful, of the fine flour of the meal offering, and of the oil thereof, and all the frankincense which is upon the meal offering, and shall burn it upon the altar for a sweet savor, as the memorial thereof, unto Jehovah.

And that which is left thereof shall Aaron and his sons eat: it shall be eaten without leaven in a holy place; in the court of the tent of the meeting they shall eat it.

It shall not be baken with leaven. I have given it as their portion of my offerings made by fire; it is most holy, as the sin offering, and as the trespass offering.

Every male among the children of Aaron shall eat of it, as his portion for ever throughout your generations, from the offerings of Jehovah made by fire: whosoever toucheth them shall be holy.

And Jehovah spake unto Moses, saying,

This is the oblation of Aaron and of his sons, which they shall offer unto Jehovah in the day when he is anointed; the tenth part of an ephah of fine flour for a meal-offering perpetually, half of it in the morning, and half thereof in the evening.

On a baking pan it shall be made with oil; when it is soaked, thou shalt bring it in: in baken pieces shalt thou offer the meal offering for a sweet savor unto Jehovah.

And the anointed priest that shall be in his stead from among his sons shall offer it: by a statute for ever it shall be wholly burnt unto Jehovah."

And every meal-offering of the priest shall be wholly burnt: it shall not be eaten."

See (P) Nu. 15 1-10

Jealousy offering.

(P) Nu. 5 12-31

II

OBJECTS USED FOR SACRIFICE

Historical Note

A. *Human Sacrifices.*

The sacrifice of human beings was common among all primitive races. It was practiced among the ancient Greeks, the Carthaginians, and the Canaanites, the pre-Hebraic inhabitants of Palestine. Abraham thought he was commanded by God to sacrifice Isaac.

(J) Gen. 22.

Recent archæological excavations have shown that at Megiddo a fifteen year old girl was placed alive in the corner stone of a house for the supposed blessing this would bring. It is a common superstition in the East that every house must have its death, either a man, a woman, a child or an animal. Every place had its god or indwelling divinity and this god must be appeased. It is said that at the opening of an electric light plant recently at Damascus an Arab Sheik sacrificed a sheep to the god of the place.

The custom must have been common, for prohibitions of human sacrifice are frequent in the Old Testament.

(H) Lev. 18 21

"And thou shalt not give any of thy seed to make them pass through the fire to Molech; neither shalt thou profane the name of thy God: I am Jehovah."

(H) Lev. 20 2-3

"Moreover, thou shalt say to the children of Israel, Whosoever he be of the children of Israel, or of the strangers that sojourn in Israel, that giveth of his seed unto Molech; he shall surely be put to death: the people of the land shall stone him with stones.

"I also will set my face against that man, and will cut him off from among his people; because he hath given of his seed unto Molech, to defile my sanctuary, and to profane my holy name."

(P) Ex. 13 [1. 2. 12.]

1 K. 16 [34]

"In his days did Hiel the Bethelite build Jericho: he laid the foundation thereof with the loss of Abiram his firstborn, and set up the gates thereof with the loss of his youngest son Segub, according to the word of Jehovah, which he spake by Joshua the son of Nun."

2 K. 3 [27]

"Then he took his eldest son that should have reigned in his stead, and offered him for a burnt offering upon the wall. And there was great wrath against Israel: and they departed from him, and returned to their own land."

2 K. 16 [3]

Jer. 7 [31. 32.]

Micah 6 [7]

(D) Dt. 18 [10]

Redemption of first born sons.

(J) Ex. 13 [15]

"And it came to pass, when Pharaoh would hardly let us go, that Jehovah slew all the firstborn in the land of Egypt, both the firstborn of man, and the firstborn of beast: therefore I sacrifice to Jehovah all that openeth the womb, being males; but all the firstborn of my sons I redeem."

See

Ju. 11 [30-40]

Mr. H. G. Wells in his *Outline of History,* quoting from the speculations of different authors, suggests that human sacrifice may have originated from the burial of the dead. When the earliest excavations were made by prehistoric man for the purpose of burying a dead body, it was necessary to disturb the soil over a considerable space. As it was their custom to leave with the body some grains of cereal to provide it with food, later they saw an abundant crop of this grain, much greater in amount than in other places, springing out of this cultivated soil. The idea no doubt occurred to the superstitious that in some way the dead body gave this greater harvest. And it was but a step to the further conclusion that human sacrifice was beneficial in producing crops of grain. In the spring when the great crop growing time arrived some human being would be killed to procure especial favor for an abundant harvest. And when the golden grain was gathered human sacrifice was again made by some tribes in gratitude it would seem for blessings received.

B. *Animal Sacrifices.*

(P) Lev. 3 [1-5]

"And if his oblation be a sacrifice of peace offerings: if he offer of the herd, whether male or female, he shall offer it without blemish before Jehovah.

And he shall lay his hand upon the head of his oblation, and kill it at the door of the tent of the meeting: and Aaron's sons the priests shall sprinkle the blood upon the altar round about.

And he shall offer of the sacrifice of peace offerings an offering made by fire unto Jehovah; the fat that covereth the inwards, and all the fat that is upon the inwards, and the two kidneys, and the fat that is on them, which is by the loins, and the caul upon the liver, with the kidneys, shall he take away.

And Aaron's sons shall burn it on the altar upon the burnt offering, which is upon the wood that is on the fire: it is an offering made by fire, of a sweet savor unto Jehovah."

(D) Dt. 12 [11]
15 [19-23]

"All the firstling males that are born of thy herd and of thy flock thou shalt sanctify unto Jehovah thy God: thou shalt do no work with the firstling of thy herd, noı shear the firstling of thy flock.

Thou shalt eat it before Jehovah thy God year by year in the place which Jehovah shall choose, thou and thy household.

And if it have any blemish, as if it be lame, or blind, any ill blemish whatsoever, thou shalt not sacrifice it unto Jehovah thy God.

Thou shalt eat it within thy gates: the unclean and the clean shall eat it alike, as the gazelle, and as the hart.

Only thou shalt not eat the blood thereof; thou shalt pour it out upon the ground as water."

(D) Dt. 17 [1]
(H) Lev. 22 [18-30]
(J) Gen. 8 [20]

"And Noah buided an altar unto Jehovah, and took of every clean beast, and of every clean bird, and offered burnt-offerings on the altar."

(C) Ex. 20 [24]

"An altar of earth thou shalt make unto me, and shalt sacrifice thereon thy burnt-offerings, and thy peace-offerings, thy sheep, and thine oxen: in every place where I record my name I will come unto thee, and I will bless thee."

(D) Dt. 12 [11-27a.]
27 [6]
1 S. 16 [2]

Redemption of firstborn.

(J) Ex. 13 [13]

For the poor turtle doves or pigeons may be offered.

(P) Lev. 5 [7]
Lev. 5 [11-13]

C. *Cereals and Libations.*

(C) Ex. 23 [18a.]
34 [25a.]

29 [41. 42]
(P) Lev. 6 [19-23]
2
23 [13]
(P) Nu. 15 [1-16]

D. *Shewbread.*

(H) Lev. 24 [5-9]

"And thou shalt take fine flour, and bake twelve cakes thereof: two tenth parts of an ephah shall be in one cake.

And thou shalt set them in two rows, six on a row, upon the pure table before Jehovah.

And thou shalt put pure frankincense upon each row, that it may be to the bread for a memorial, even an offering made by fire unto Jehovah.

Every sabbath he shall set it in order before Jehovah continually; it is on behalf of the children of Israel, an everlasting covenant.

And it shall be for Aaron and his sons; and they shall eat it in a holy place: for it is most holy unto him of the offerings of Jehovah made by fire by a perpetual statute."

(P) Ex. 25 [30]

E. *Sacred Lamps and Incense.*

(H) Lev. 24 [1-4]

"And the Lord spake unto Moses, saying,

Command the children of Israel, that they bring unto thee pure olive oil beaten for the light, to cause a lamp to burn continually.

Without the veil of the testimony, in the tent of the meeting, shall Aaron order it from evening to morning before Jehovah continually: it shall be a statute for ever throughout your generations.

He shall order the lamps upon the pure candlestick before Jehovah continually."

(P) Ex. 30 [7-9. 34. 35]

The expiatory character of sacrifices is indicated by the following—God must be propitiated.

1 S. 3[14]
1 S. 26[19]
2 S. 24[25]
Mic. 6[6. 7.]

Sacrifice considered a gift to God.

(C) Ex. 23[15]
34[20]

As food.

(P) Lev. 3[11]

"And the priest shall burn it upon the altar: it is the food of the offering made by fire unto Jehovah."

(H) Lev. 21[8. 21]
1 S. 21[4-6] 26[19]
(P) Nu. 28[2]
Ezek. 44[7]

III

RITUAL OF SACRIFICES

At first no priest was required. The worshiper killed his own animal.

(J) Gen. 22[9]
1 S. 14[33. 34.]

When the elaborate ritual of the temple was devised priests became necessary. The ceremony for each kind of beast or offering was minutely prescribed and must be carried out with the most scrupulous care for details. The Priestly Code contains these various rites, all of which were regarded as of the utmost importance. The priest thus acquired increased dignity and importance in the Jewish ceremonial.

The animal sacrificed must not be blemished.

(D) Dt. 17[1]

Worshipers must first sanctify themselves, by washing or changing garments.

1 S. 16[5]
(E) Ex. 19[10. 11.]

The blood must never be eaten, for "the blood is the life," and life came from God.

1 S. 14 [34]

(H) Lev. 17 [11]

"For the life of the flesh is in the blood; and I have given it to you upon the altar to make an atonement for your souls; for it is the blood that maketh atonement by reason of the life."

(C) Ex. 23 [18.]

For full description of the ceremony of burnt offering, meal offering, and peace offering see

(P) Lev. Chs. 1. 2. 3.
Lev. 6 [8-23]
7 [8-18]
(P) Nu. 15 [2-13]

(1) *For sin offerings.*

(P) Lev. Chs. 4 & 5 [1-13]
6 [24-30]

(2) *The trespass offerings.*

(P) Lev. 5 [14-19]
6 [1-7]
7 [1-7]

(3) *Heave and Wave Offering.*

(H) Lev. 23 [10-13] [17-21]
(P) Nu. 15 [19-21]

(4) *For the share of the priests.*

(P) Lev. 7 [28-36]
(P) Nu. 18 [9-19]
See 1 S. 2 [13-16]
(P) Nu. 31 [25-31]
(D) Dt. 18 [3. 4.]

(5) *Share of Levites from local churches to temple at Jerusalem.*

(D) Dt. 18 [6-8]

(6) *For full Ritual* see

(P) Lev. 9
24 [2-4]

Salt was a necessary ingredient.

(P) Lev. 2 [13]

Mk. 9 [49]

(7) For the special elaborate ritual for the *Day of Atonement* see

(P) Lev. 16

C

TITHES AND DUES

DUES

Historical Note

The first-born son of a Jewish household belonged to Jehovah. That was His "due." The most precious thing which a man had to give was required of him as a member of the sacred race. In the very earliest times it appeared that this son was actually sacrificed as a victim to Jehovah. This was abolished, however, and the first-born of the flocks and herds, the first fruits of the land were substituted. There was an elaborate ritual prescribed for the redemption of the first-born son, which involved the payment of a stipulated sum as ransom.

(1) First-born Sons.

(J) See (E) Gen. 22
(P) Ex. 13 [1. 2. 15]
(C) Ex. 22 [29b.]

"The first-born of thy sons shalt thou give unto me."

(J) Ex. 34 [19a]
(P) Nu. 8 [16. 17.]

For redemption of first-born son see

(J) Ex. 34 [20c.]
(P) Nu. 3 [11-13 44-51]
8 [18]
8 [18]

Provision was made to prevent extortion.

(P) Lev. 27 [8]

(2) First-born of flocks and herds.

(J) Ex. 13 [11-13a.]

(C) 22 [30]

"Likewise shalt thou do with thine oxen, and with thy sheep: seven days it shall be with his dam; on the eighth day thou shalt give it me."

(J) Ex. 34 [19b. 20]

(P) Lev. 27 [26. 27]

(P) Nu. 18 [15. 17.]

"Everything that openeth the womb of all flesh which they offer unto Jehovah, both of man and beast, shall be thine: nevertheless the first-born of man shalt thou surely redeem, and the firstling of unclean beasts shalt thou redeem."

But the firstling of a cow, or the firstling of a sheep, or the firstling of a goat, thou shalt not redeem; they are holy; thou shalt sprinkle their blood upon the altar, and shalt burn their fat for an offering made by fire, for a sweet savor unto Jehovah."

(D) Dt. 14 [23b.]

15 [19-22]

(3) Redemption by payment of money was provided if the worshiper resided too far from Jerusalem to take his offering to the temple.

(D) Dt. 14 [24-26]

"And if the way be too long for thee, so that thou art not able to carry it, because the place is too far from thee, which Jehovah thy God shall choose, to set his name there, when Jehovah thy God shall bless thee: then shalt thou turn it into money, and bind up the money in thy hand, and shalt go unto the place which Jehovah thy God shall choose: and thou shalt bestow the money for whatsoever thy soul desireth, for oxen, or for sheep, or for wine, or for strong drink, or for whatsoever thy soul asketh of thee: and thou shalt eat there before Jehovah thy God, and thou shalt rejoice, thou, and thy household."

(4) First Fruits.

(C) Ex. 23 [19a.]

"The first of the first fruits of thy ground thou shalt bring into the house of Jehovah thy God."

(J) Ex. 34 [26a.]
(H) Lev. 19 [24]
23 [10. 11]
(P) Nu. 15 [17-21]
(D) Dt. 18 [4]
26 [1-11]

(5) Tithes.

The system of tithing—or the gift of one-tenth of the income, was common in Babylonia, Egypt, Carthage and Syria as well as among the Hebrews. It first appears in the Old Testament in Amos 4 [4], thus dating to at least 800 B. C. In two out of three years the tithe was taken to the temple at Jerusalem. The third year it was given to the needy. Later the tithe was rigidly enforced.

(P) Lev. 27 [30-32]

"And all the tithe of the land, whether of the seed of the land, or of the fruit of the tree, is Jehovah's: it is holy unto Jehovah.

And if a man will redeem aught of his tithe, he shall add unto it the fifth part thereof.

And all the tithe of the herd, or of the flock, whatsoever passeth under the rod, the tenth shall be holy unto Jehovah."

(P) Nu. 18 [25. 26.]
(D) Dt. 14 [22-27]
26 [12. 13]
(E) Gen. 28 [20-22]

"And Jacob vowed a vow, saying, If God will be with me, and will keep me in this way that I go, and will give me bread to eat, and raiment to put on, so that I come again to my father's house in peace, and Jehovah will be my God, then this stone, which I have set for a pillar, shall be God's house: and of all that thou shalt give me I will surely give the tenth unto thee."

Redemption of tithe.

(P) Lev. 27 [33]

The tithe was originally a gift to the Levites in place of their inheritance which was denied them upon the allotment of the land of Canaan.

(P) Nu. 18 [21-24]

"And, unto the children of Levi, behold, I have given all the tithe in Israel for an inheritance, in return for their service which they serve, even the service of the tent of the meeting.

And henceforth the children of Israel shall not come nigh the tent of the meeting, lest they bear sin, and die.

But, the Levites shall do the service of the tent of the meeting, and they shall bear their iniquity: it shall be a statute for ever throughout your generations; and among the children of Israel they shall have no inheritance.

For the tithe of the children of Israel, which they offer as a heave offering unto Jehovah, I have given to the Levites for an inheritance therefore I have said unto them, Among the children of Israel they shall have no inheritance."

(6) Poll Tax.

(P) Ex. 30 [11-16]

D

PERSONS VOWED OR DEVOTED AND THINGS SACRIFICED

According to the ancient custom a man could vow or devote himself or sanctify some possession of value to Jehovah, and this had all the validity of a contract. Thenceforth the person or thing vowed or devoted belonged to the Sanctuary. If property it was used for the priests who received their support in this way out of tithes, dues and things sanctified. If a person wished to redeem himself or withdraw the property from this use, it was usual to allow "redemption" by paying a sum "estimated" by the priests plus twenty per cent. The full schedule of valuation for persons and different articles is found in

(P) Lev. 27 [1-29]
(P) Nu. 30 [2-15]
See also (D) Dt. 12 [26. 6]
23 [21-23]
(H) Lev. 22 [21]
(D) Dt. 16 [10]
As to Nazarites see
(P) Nu. 6 [2-21]

E

CLEAN AND UNCLEAN

Introductory Note

The Jews were no exception to the universal rule among primitive peoples that certain things were regarded as sacred and some were to be shunned. Speaking in terms of ceremony things were considered as clean and unclean. The word taboo is used to express the latter. No doubt the origin of taboo was in fear. People believed that every object had an indwelling spirit, and if this spirit was an evil one the thing must be shunned or propitiated. An illustration of this is the belief that "the blood is the life," hence the sternest commands against its use. In many cases there seems to be no logical basis for belief that a certain thing was taboo. Objects of taboo varied in different countries. Perhaps a fuller knowledge of primitive psychology will throw light on this difficult question. It is impossible to give here a comprehensive discussion of the subject. It is recommended that the matter be studied more fully in the Cyclopedias.

Attention may be called, however, to one or two special

topics. It is probable the law of clean and unclean was in fact founded on hygienic reasons. Many of the rules conform to the best modern scientific knowledge, others are apparently baseless. If carefully complied with they were at least a measure of safety in times and among people of the profoundest ignorance as to science.

Meat killed in accordance with Jewish rules, including among others that animals should be killed with a knife and the blood carefully drained is called Kosher and the prescribed rules are still in full force and practice among orthodox Jews the world over.

1. For full rules regarding clean and unclean see:—

(1) *Unclean food.*

(P) Lev. 11
(D) Dt. 14
Mk. 7 [1-4]

Rules against eating blood.

(H) Lev. 19 [26]
(D) Dt. 12 [23]
15 [23]
1 Sam. 14 [32-35]

Further see

(P) Gen. 9 [4]
(H) Lev. 19 [26a. 5-8]
(P) 3 [17]
7 [15-19 23b.-26]
17 [10-14]
(C) Ex. 23 [19]
34 [26b.]
(D) Dt. 12 [16.]

(2) *Animals torn or dead shall not be eaten.*

(C) Ex. 22 [31]

"And ye shall be holy men unto me: therefore ye shall not eat any flesh that is torn of beasts in the field; ye shall cast it to the dogs."

(P) Lev. 7 [24] 17 [15]
(H) Lev. 22 [8]

(D) Dt. 14^{21}

(3) *Leavened bread.*

(P) Ex. 12$^{18-20}$

"In the first month, on the fourteenth day of the month at even, ye shall eat unleavened bread, until the one and twentieth day of the month at even.

Seven days shall there be no leaven found in your houses: for whosoever eateth that which is leavened, that soul shall be cut off from the congregation of Israel, whether he be a sojourner, or one that is born in the land.

Ye shall eat nothing leavened; in all your habitations shall ye eat unleavened bread."

(C) Ex. 23^{18}
(J) 34$^{25a.}$

(4) *Unleavened bread.*

(J) Ex. 13$^{6. 7.}$
(H) Lev. 23^{6}
Jos. 5^{11}

(5) *The Fruit of Young Trees.*

(H) Lev. 19$^{23-25}$

(6) *Contact with unclean things.*
With the dead.

(D) Dt. 21$^{22. 23}$
(H) Lev. 22$^{4a. 6b.}$
(P) 5^{2} 11^{8}
(P) Nu. 19$^{11-21}$
9$^{10-12}$
31^{19}

With unclean things.

(P) Nu. 19^{22}

"And whatsoever the unclean person toucheth shall be unclean; and the soul that toucheth it shall be unclean until even."

(P) Lev. 5$^{3.}$ 7$^{19-27}$
11$^{24. 25. 39. 40.}$ 15$^{1-33}$ 21$^{4-6}$

(7) *With the Spoils of War.*

(P) Nu. 31$^{20-24}$

(8) *As to Nazarites.*
(P) Nu. 6 [1-12]

(9) *By Touching Holy Things.*
(H) Lev. 22 [3. 14]

(10) *Against Defiling for the Dead.*
(H) Lev. 21 [1-3]

(11) *By Priest.*
(H) Lev. 21 [10-12]

2. CAUSES OF UNCLEANNESS

(1) *Loathsome diseases.*
(D) Dt. 24 [8]

(2) *Leprosy.*
(P) Lev. 13

(3) *Issue of blood.*
(P) Lev. 15 [2b.-16 19-26]

(4) *Intercourse.*
(P) Lev. 15 [16-18] 18 [20]

(5) *Female Impurity.*
(P) Lev. 15 [19-30] 18 [19]

(6) *Childbirth.*
(P) Lev. 12 [1. 2. 4. 5.]

3. MANNER OF RESTORING CEREMONIAL CLEANLINESS

The usual methods enjoined to remove ceremonial uncleanness were the use of water for washing, bathing, etc., and an act of sacrifice. In certain cases such as leprosy there were added entire isolation of the person affected, fumigation, removal of infected objects, replastering the house, and in extreme cases its complete destruction. In some cases burning was required. These methods were as efficient as we might expect in an age ignorant of sanitation and medical science. Some of the various rules to restore cleanliness are here given.

(P) Lev. 12 [6. 8.]
11 [25. 40.]

"And whosoever beareth aught of the carcass of them shall wash his clothes, and be unclean until the even.

And he that eateth of the carcass of it shall wash his clothes, and be unclean until the even: he also that beareth the carcass of it shall wash his clothes, and be unclean until the even."

(D) Dt. 14
(P) Lev. 13 [45-59]
14 [1-57]
15 [2-33]
(P) Nu. 19 [12. 17-19]

Kinds of offerings.

(H) Lev. 22 [17-30]

F

CIRCUMCISION

Circumcision was common in ancient times among Western Semites. It may have originated in hygienic reasons, or possibly may have been a survival of phallic worship. According to Herodotus it was in use among the Egyptians.

Among the Jews circumcision was regarded as of the most profound importance. It was the distinguishing mark of the race—that which set them apart as a holy nation. The custom has been universally followed and is to this day observed in Jewish households.

Origin and Rules.

(P) Gen. 17 [9-14]
21 [4]
(P) Ex. 12 [48]
(P) Lev. 12 [3]

G

SACRED PLACES

Historical Note

The places where men worship have always been regarded as sacred. In these places God is supposed to have "set his name" and to be present in an especial sense. The worshiper could there come into direct contact with Deity and his worship would be especially efficacious. To make such places convenient of access would be to multiply acts of worship and tend to bind Jehovah and his people together. In early Jewish history places of special historic or religious interest such as Bethel and Shiloh were designated by Jehovah and worship commanded in them.

At the time of the tremendous revolution in Jewish worship and ritual effected by the Book of the Law in 621 B. C. grave abuses had grown up around these Special Sanctuaries or "high places" and in accordance with drastic commands they were all destroyed. All Jewish worship thereafter centered at Jerusalem which became in a double sense a sacred city. The student must bear constantly in mind this distinction between modes of worship prior to and after this epoch making event.

The Worship of the Jews consisted almost wholly of sacrifices. These represented the attitude of submission on the part of the worshiper and an objective mode of securing the favor of his Deity. Acts were right or wrong not because of any innate quality in themselves, or of man's duty to his fellow man, but because God commanded or prohibited them.

But the moral element in religion, conduct rather than sacrifice, was preached eloquently by the great prophets. See

Is. 1 11-17

"What unto me is the multitude of your sacrifices? saith Jehovah: I have had enough of the burnt-offerings of rams, and the fat of fed beasts; and I delight not in the blood of bullocks, or of lambs, or of he-goats.

When ye come to appear before me, who hath required this at your hand, to trample my courts?

Bring no more vain oblations; incense is an abomination unto me; new moons and sabbath, the calling of assemblies,—I cannot away with iniquity, and the solemn meeting.

Your new moons and your appointed feasts my soul hateth: they are a trouble unto me; I am weary of bearing them.

And when ye spread forth your hands, I will hide mine eyes from you; yea, when ye make many prayers, I will not hear: your hands are full of blood.

Wash you, make you clean; put away the evil of your doings from before mine eyes; cease to do evil; learn to do well; seek justice, relieve the oppressed, judge the fatherless, plead for the widow."

Mic. 6 6-8

"Wherewith shall I come before Jehovah, and bow myself before the high God? shall I come before him with burnt-offerings, with calves a year old?

Will Jehovah be pleased with thousands of rams, or with ten thousands of rivers of oil? Shall I give my firstborn for my transgression, the fruit of my body for the sin of my soul?

He hath showed thee, O man, what is good; and what doth Jehovah require of thee, but to do justly, and to love kindness, and to walk humbly with thy God?"

It must not be forgotten, however, that the great prophets did not oppose ritual, they blamed the priests not for observing the sacred rites, but for making these superior in importance to moral instruction. In all ages there is this eternal conflict between the prophet who magnifies life and conduct, and the priest who places chief stress upon the outward observance of rites and ceremonies.

The Jewish race was to the time of Christ a race of ceremonialists. The priests exerted greater influence over them than the prophets. Jesus rebuked the Pharisees for paying more attention to "tithing mint and anise than the weightier matters of the law."

Attention has been called before to the primitive idea that each spot had its indwelling spirit. It was also a common belief that certain places were especially sacred and that by appropriate ceremony this sacred character could be imparted. Such were places where Jehovah "put his name." We shall readily understand the following references by bearing these facts constantly in mind.

1. *Ancient Altars Commanded.*

(C) Ex. 20^{24-26}

"An altar of earth thou shalt make unto me, and shalt sacrifice thereon thy burnt-offerings, and thy peace offerings, thy sheep, and thine oxen: in every place where I record my name I will come unto thee, and I will bless thee.

And if thou make me an altar of stone, thou shalt not build it of hewn stones; for if thou lift up thy tool upon it, thou hast polluted it.

Neither shalt thou go up by steps unto mine altar, that thy nakedness be not uncovered thereon."

(D) Dt. $27^{5-8\ 2.\ 3.}$

Destruction of High Places Ordered.

(D) Dt. 12^{2-3}

"Ye shall surely destroy all the places wherein the nations that ye shall dispossess served their gods, upon the high mountains, and upon the hills, and under every green tree: and ye shall break down their altars, and dash in pieces their pillars, and burn their asherim with fire; and ye shall hew down the graven images of their gods; and ye shall destroy their name out of that place."

2 K. 22^{8}
23$^{4-20}$

These references should be read in full carefully. They demonstrate that the Deuteronomic Code was the Book of the Law found by Hilkiah the high priest in the Temple and the authorship of which was for obvious reasons ascribed to Moses.

2. *The Ark of the Covenant.*

(D) Dt. 10$^{1-5}$
31$^{25-26}$
(P) Ex. 25$^{10-40}$
(P) Ex. 26$^{34-37}$
27$^{1-8}$ 37$^{1-9}$
30$^{1-6\ 17-21}$
(P) Nu. 8^{4}
10$^{33-36}$

The tables of stone on which the law was written were placed in the Ark. That the Jews needed this visible proof of Jehovah's presence illustrates their primitive conceptions. They had scarcely yet passed the anthropomorphic stage.

The Altar.

(P) Ex. 30$^{1-10}$
36^{25}

The Mercy Seat.

(P) Ex. 25^{17}

Cherubim.

(P) Ex. 25^{18}

3. *The Tabernacle or Tent of the Meeting.*

The Tent of the Meeting was a simple structure which could be quickly and easily moved from place to place. The Tabernacle was more substantial and was suited to less nomadic habits.

(P) Ex. 26$^{1-37}$
27$^{1-19}$
25$^{1-9,\ 22}$
33$^{5-11}$

Ex. 30
31^{1-11}
36^{8} 38^{20}

4. *Different Sanctuaries Established.*

(D) Dt. 12^{10-18}

"But when ye go over the Jordan, and dwell in the land which Jehovah your God causeth you to inherit, and he giveth you rest from all your enemies round about, so that ye dwell in safety: then it shall come to pass that to the place which Jehovah your God shall choose, to cause his name to dwell there, thither shall ye bring all that I command you; your burnt-offerings, and your sacrifices, your tithes, and the heave-offering of your hand, and all your choice vows which ye vow unto Jehovah.

And ye shall rejoice before Jehovah your God, ye, and your sons, and your daughters, and your menservants, and your maidservants, and the Levite that is within your gates, forasmuch as he hath no portion nor inheritance with you.

Take heed to thyself that thou offer not thy burnt-offerings in every place that thou seest: but in the place which Jehovah shall choose in one of thy tribes, there thou shalt offer thy burnt-offerings, and there thou shalt do all that I command thee.

Notwithstanding, thou mayest kill and eat flesh in all thy gates, after all the desire of thy soul, according to the blessing of Jehovah thy God which he hath given thee: the unclean and the clean may eat thereof, as of the gazelle, and as of the hart.

Only ye shall not eat the blood; ye shall pour it upon the earth as water.

Thou mayest not eat within thy gates the tithe of thy grain, or of thy new wine, or of thine oil, or the firstlings of thy herds or of thy flock, nor any of thy vows which thou vowest, nor thy free will offerings, nor heave-offering of thy hand: but thou shalt eat them before Jehovah thy God in the place which Jehovah thy God shall choose, thou, and thy son, and thy daughter, and thy manservant, and thy maidservant, and the Levite that is within thy gates: and thou shalt rejoice before Jehovah thy God in all that thou puttest thy hand unto."

(D) Dt. 14 [22-26]
15 [19. 20]
16 [5-7]
31 [10. 11.]

5. *Solomon's Temple.*

1 K. 6 [2-38]
7 [1-45]
2 Chr. 3 [1-17]
4 [1-22]
5 [1]

6. *Ezekiel's Temple.*

Ezek. Chs. 40 to 46

H

SACRED OFFICIALS

In the earliest times and for many centuries the father of a family acted as priest for his household. He killed the animal, poured out its blood, burned its fat, and offered it to Jehovah. The following incidents illustrate the rule.

Gideon—Judges 6 [26]
Saul—1 Sam. 14 [34. 35.]
Solomon—1 K. 8 [5. 62 64.]
9 [25]

Priests officiated at the High Places scattered over the country, but when the entire worship of the nation was centered at Jerusalem an elaborate organization sprang up, and the priesthood became hereditary.

1

Priests, Levites, High Priests

Originally Aaron and his sons were the priests. These were to perform the sacred rites upon the altar and have charge of the same.

The Levites were members of the tribe of Levi. Their duty was to have charge of the tabernacle or tent of the meeting and to serve as helpers to the priests. Later the distinction seems to have disappeared.

(D) Dt. 21[5]
27[9]

(1) *Appointment of Aaron and sons to priesthood.*

(P) Nu. 3[2. 3. 10.]
(P) Ex. 28[1]
30[30]

(2) *Their consecration.*

(P) Lev. 8[1-36]
(P) Ex. 29[1-44]
39[27-29]
40[12-15]

"And thou shalt bring Aaron and his sons unto the door of the tent of the meeting, and shalt wash them with water.

And thou shalt put upon Aaron the holy garments; and thou shalt anoint him, and sanctify him, that he may minister unto me in the priest's office.

And thou shalt bring his sons, and put coats upon them; and thou shalt anoint them, as thou didst anoint their father, that they may minister unto me in the priest's office: and their anointing shall be to them for an everlasting priesthood throughout their generations."

(3) *Appointment of Levites.*

(P) Nu. 3[45.5-39]
(P) Nu. 8[15. 19. 24. 25.]
1[47-53]

18 [2-7]
(P) Ex. 32 [29]
(D) Dt. 10 [8. 9.]
21 [5b.]

(4) *Their consecration.*
(P) Nu. 8 [6-12]

No person having a blemish could be a priest.
(H) Lev. 21 [17-23]

(5) *Ceremonial Cleanliness of Priests.*
(P) Ex. 28 [40-43]
29 [8. 9.]
30 [17-21]
(P) Lev. 8 [13] 10 [6-10]
19 [27. 28]
21 [1-7]
22 [1-9]

(6) *Duties and Authority of Priests.*
(P) Nu. 10 [8-10]
18 [1-7]
(P) Lev. 2 [1. 2. 9. 14-16]
6 [6. 7. 13. 14.]
(D) Dt. 20 [2-4] 21 [5]

To act as judges.
(C) Ex. 21 [22] 22 [8. 9.]
(D) Dt. 17 [8-13]

Under Ezekiel.
Ezek. Chs. 44-48

Of Levites.
(P) Nu. 3 [5-9]
3 [14-51]
4 [1-49]
8 [14-26]
18 [21-24]
(D) Dt. 24 [8]
33 [8a. 10]
1 Ch. 23 [1-32]

To act as judges.

2 Ch. 19^{8-11}

(D) Dt. 17^{8-13}

But the Levites lost their position as judges after the exile.

(7) *Support of Priests.*

(P) Lev. 27^{30-33}

(P) Nu. 18^{9-19}

(P) Ex. 29^{26-28}

"And thou shalt take the breast of Aaron's ram of consecration, and wave it for a wave-offering before Jehovah: and it shall be thy portion.

And thou shalt sanctify the breast of the wave-offering, and the thigh of the heave-offering, which is waved, and which is heaved up, of the ram of the consecration, even of that which is for Aaron, and of that which is for his sons: and it shall be for Aaron and his sons as their portion for ever from the children of Israel; for it is a heave-offering: and it shall be a heave-offering from the children of Israel of the sacrifices of their peace-offerings, even their heave-offering unto Jehovah."

(P) Lev. 2^{3}

5^{13}

(P) Lev. 6^{24-26}

10^{12-19}

14^{13}

23^{5-20}

24^{5-9}

27^{1-33}

Mk. 2^{26}

(P) Nu. 3^{46-51}

"And for the redemption of the two hundred and threescore and thirteen of the firstborn of the children of Israel, that are over and above the number of the Levites, thou shalt take five shekels apiece by the poll; after the shekel of the sanctuary shalt thou take them: (the shekel is twenty gerahs:) and thou shalt give the money, wherewith the odd number of them is redeemed, unto Aaron and to his sons.

And Moses took the redemption-money of them that were over and above them that were redeemed by the Levites: from the firstborn of the children of Israel took he the money; a thousand three hundred and threescore and five shekels, after the shekel of the sanctuary; and Moses gave the redemption money unto Aaron and to his sons, according to the word of Jehovah, as Jehovah commanded Moses."

(P) Nu. 5 [6-10]
6 [19. 20]
15 [20. 21]
31 [25-29]

Support of Levites.

(D) Dt. 14 [28. 29]
(D) Dt. 14 [27]
18 [1-8]
(P) Nu. 18 [21-31]
31 [30. 47.]
35 [1-8]

The wages of prostitution could not be used for the support of priests.

(D) Dt. 23 [18]

2

The High Priests

This was a post-exilic title. The complete hierarchy was then as follows:

1. The High Priest.
2. His kinsman and associates, that is, the sons of Aaron, which included the Zadokites.
3. The Levites who performed the menial duties.

(a) *Installation.*

(P) Ex. 29 [5-7]
40 [12-13]
(P) Lev. 8 [7-12]

(b) *Clothing.*

(P) Ex. 28 [1-39]
29 [29. 30.]
39 [1. 31.]
(P) Lev. 8 [7-12]

(c) *Ceremonial Cleanliness.*

(P) Lev. 10 [8. 9.]
21 [10-15]

(d) *Duties.*

(P) Ex. 28 [29-30]
30 [7. 8. 10.]

"And Aaron shall burn thereon incense of sweet spices: every morning, when he dresseth the lamps, he shall burn it.

And when Aaron lighteth the lamps at even, he shall burn it, a perpetual incense before Jehovah throughout your generations."

"And Aaron shall make atonement upon the horns of it once in the year; with the blood of the sin-offering of atonements once in the year shall he make atonement for it throughout your generations: it is most holy unto Jehovah."

(P) Lev. 6 [19-22]
16 [1-34]

THE END

APPENDIX

A

SELECTED BIBLIOGRAPHY

The following is not intended as a complete bibliography but as a selected and suggestive list of books which will be extremely helpful to the Bible Student, and which will be found sufficient for ordinary class work.

American Revised Version of the Bible.
Apocrypha.
Hasting's Dictionary of the Bible.
Young's or Cruden's Concordance.
Encyc. Britannica. Special Articles.
Jewish Cyclopedia.
Encyclopedia of Religion and Ethics.
Driver's Introduction to the Literature of the Old Testament.
Moore's History of Religions.
Hodges—How to Know the Bible.
Gladden—Who Wrote the Bible.
Kent—Historical Bible.
" Bible Geography and History.
" History of the Hebrew People.
" Origin and Permanent Value of the Old Testament.
" Israel's Laws and Legal Precedents.
Toy—History of the Religion of Israel.
Jastrow—Civilization of Babylonia and Assyria.
Barton—Archæology in Bible Lands.
Kohler—Jewish Theology.
Moulton—The Bible as Literature.
Martineau—Seat of Authority in Religion.
Johns—Translation of the Code of Hammurabi.

B

Grateful acknowledgment is made to Rev. J. T. Sunderland, D.D., from whose valuable work, *The Origin and Character of the Bible,* most of the dates contained in the following tables are taken by permission.

DATES OF BIBLICAL LITERATURE

Many of these dates are only approximate

	B. C.
The Prophetic Narrative or "Document" of the Hexateuch known to scholars as "J," compiled about . .	850–800
The Prophetic Narrative or "Document" "E," compiled about	800–750
Amos, the earliest written book of the Bible . . .	750
Documents "J" and "E" combined	650–625
Deuteronomy (Document "D") written	650–621
Discovery of the "Book of the Law" (Deuteronomy, Document "D") in the Temple	621
Jeremiah	626–580
Proverbs, earliest collection (x:1-xxii:16) perhaps .	621–600
Psalms. Many individual psalms doubtless written before the Exile. (Probably no collection made until the time of Ezra, in the fifth century) . . .	
Ezekiel	593–570
Priestly Document, "P," main parts compiled . .	560–500
The "Second Isaiah" (Isaiah xl-lv and perhaps lvi-lxvi)	540
Judges	560–500
1 and 2 Samuel	560–500
1 and 2 Kings (formerly one book)	560–500
Joshua	450–400
Job, possibly written during the Exile; more likely	450–400
Priestly Document, "P," published to the people by Ezra as the "Law of the Lord," the "Law of Moses," The "Book of the Law"	444?
Completion of the Pentateuch by a union of "J," "E," "D" and "P"	400
Genesis, in its present form	400
Exodus, in its present form	400
Leviticus, in its present form	400
Numbers, in its present form	400
Canon of "The Law" completed	400–300
Ezra in its present form, about	300
Nehemiah in its present form, about	300
1 and 2 Chronicles (originally one book)	300
Canon of "The Prophets" completed	300–200
Translation of the Old Testament into Greek by Jewish Scholars in Alexandria (the Septuagint)	250–100
	A. D.
Old Testament Canon, virtual final settlement of, by the Jews at the Synod at Jamnia	90–100

DATES OF IMPORTANT HISTORICAL EVENTS, BIBLICAL AND OTHER

Some of these dates are only approximate

Event	B. C.
In Babylonia and Egypt powerful Kingdoms and advanced Civilization as early as	5000–4000
Sargon, King of Akkad, and his son Naram-Sin, unify Babylonia and found a Semitic Empire, which includes Syria and Palestine about . . .	3800
In Egypt the great pyramid at Gizeh built by King Khufu or Cheops. The Book of the Dead written	4000–3500
Code of Hammurabi of Babylon	2250
Palestine under Babylonian rule. Much culture, largely of Babylonian origin. Babylonian script in use	2000–1500
Migrations of Semitic Tribes, ancestors of the Hebrews, giving rise to the Abraham, Jacob and Joseph stories of Genesis, possibly 2000–1600, but more likely	1700–1400
Palestine under Egyptian rule	1400
Moses, the Exodus of Israelitish tribes from Egypt about	1300
Conquest of Canaan; Government of tribes by Judges or Chiefs (Period of the Judges)	1300-1030
Samuel (Judge and Prophet). Consolidation of tribes	1050
Monarchy established. Saul the first King . . .	1030–1010
David, King	1010– 973
Solomon becomes King	973
Homeric Age in Greece . . . . . . 10th to	9th century
Solomon's Temple in Jerusalem dedicated . . .	963
Division of Kingdom into "Israel" in the North and "Judah" in the South	930
Elijah, about	860
The "Moabite Stone" believed to come from about .	850
Foundation of Rome (supposed)	753
Great Creative Age of Hebrew Prophecy (Amos, Hosea, Isaiah, and Micah)	8th century
Kingdom of "Israel" overthrown by Assyria; many taken away captives. ("Lost Tribes") . . .	721
Hezekiah's Reformation, about	715
Sennacherib of Assyria devastates much of Judah. Jerusalem saved	701
"Book of Law" discovered in Temple (followed by Josiah's Reformation)	621

Jeremiah	626– 580
Fall of Nineveh	606
Solon, in Greece	640– 559
Lao-tse, in China, latter part of	6th century
Buddha in India, possibly	623– 556
Nebuchadnezzar takes Jerusalem	597
Jerusalem destroyed; Kingdom of Judah broken up. Many Jews carried into exile in Babylonia . .	586
Babylon captured by Cyrus the Persian . . .	539
Return of Jews from exile, led by Zerubabbel . .	536
Period of Persian Rule of Palestine	536– 333
Confucius, in China	550– 478
Dedication of Second Temple in Jerusalem . .	516
Ezra comes to Palestine with many more exiles . .	458
Influence of Priests and Scribes increases, and influence of prophets declines	5th century
Synagogues multiply and grow in influence . .	4th century
Translation of Old Testament into Greek in Alexandria (the Septuagint)	250– 100

C

SUGGESTIONS TO TEACHERS OF ADULT BIBLE CLASSES

For the benefit of teachers of adult Bible classes the following suggestions are made as to the best methods of using this book for class purposes. Nothing of course can take the place of thorough preparation and personal interest on the part of the teacher. Added to these should be a knowledge of correct pedagogical principles and of psychology. Thorough information alone will not take the place of skill and understanding as to how knowledge is to be imparted and the mind aroused to think and investigate for itself.

1. There should be thorough mastery of materials, a thorough understanding as to each subject treated and the reasons for its separate classification and analysis.
2. The teacher should have a general view of Jewish History and of the structure and make-up of the Bible. To this end there should be study of the results of the Higher Criticism as applied to the books, composition, dates and authorship of the Old Testament.
3. The teacher should give his classes a proper idea of the place of the Torah, or the Jewish Law, in comparison with the other divisions and parts of the Bible.
4. Teach by topics. Each subject or branch of the Law should

be studied vertically, rather than horizontally. What is meant is that a definite topic, such for instance as the law of Real Estate, should be traced from its earliest beginnings down through various stages of Jewish history, showing the changes and developments that came with varying conditions of national life. A study of all phases of society that are contemporaneous may be of value for many purposes, indeed indispensable for an exact picture of life at any definite period. But for a detailed study of laws it is preferable to take up each subject topically and trace its origin, development and final form.

5. Of vital importance and the purpose to which this book is primarily dedicated, is to correlate the various ancient laws with modern laws and regulations on the same subject. This and this alone gives the study of Jewish law that freshness and interest which will make it of value. The wide-awake teacher will find on every page suggestions as to parallel laws in our modern codes. A comparison of these, with a discussion of the reasons for such parallelism, will be found of the most intense interest, and of profound value by way of observation, and reasoning on social and economic subjects. Incidentally it will also demonstrate how causes operated in that ancient world similar to those we observe all about us to-day, a valuable lesson in sociology.

6. It is scarcely necessary to emphasize the thought that the fundamental reason for Bible study is religious instruction. Any inquiry into ancient life has a certain cultural value, but it is the religious and moral element alone that justifies intensive study of the Old Testament. To learn how to live is more important than any knowledge of dry historical facts.

7. Frequent illustrations from science, literature and history should be used. Many students would be attracted by these collateral illustrations who would be unable to follow a strict adherence to the text. As an example, discuss the geological record of the earth's history in connection with the stories of Creation in Genesis. The bearing of Evolution on the doctrine of the Fall of Man will be apparent. The place of sacrifices in all religions will throw light on the various doctrines as to the Atonement. Astronomy, mathematics, biology, sociology, ethics may all contribute subject matter for discussion on various questions of theology, of religious observances, of legal regulations.

It follows that the wider the preparation and knowledge of the teacher the greater his opportunity to make the study of the Bible living and vital.

8. The teacher should emphasize the great relative value of the Old Testament as the foundation of our Christian System of

religion. The wonderful story of the Jewish genius for religion, the high moral standards, the advanced regulations, the origin of Monotheism, the marvelous literature, these may all be woven into the study of Jewish Law and be made of entrancing interest.

9. A comparative study of Jewish law with that of other nations, for instance Babylonia and Egypt, and especially the Code of Hammurabi, will be found profitable and will widen the outlook of the scholars. A careful study of the bibliography in the appendix will disclose much valuable material.

10. Archæology has become a wonderful field of study in recent years. Our leading newspapers and magazines contribute from time to time items of much interest concerning recent discoveries. By keeping up to date with current explorations a fascination may be added to the ancient story.

11. Familiar facts and illustrations from every day life and experience can be woven into the class work, for the essential study is that of life, and life is everywhere of the same texture. How we react to stimuli to-day can be referred back to ancient people with the reasonable certainty that they were affected in like manner by like causes. Personal impulses, social motives, local incidents, every day observations may be made to contribute to the lesson story.

12. Always it must be remembered it is a vital, living, moving story we are studying, not a historical mummy that we are dissecting. Every probe goes into the sensitive, bleeding life of those people who had such an enthralling sense of the Divine presence and guidance, and who in all their experiences and institutions were intensely human.